Skip Cannon Recalls

A Lifetime of Scouting in Westmorland

Jim Cannon

Published by

H E L M
PRESS

Dedicated to the two most important women in my life,
my mother and my wife, Kirsten.

Published by Helm Press
10 Abbey Gardens, Natland, Kendal, Cumbria LA9 7SP
Tel: 015395 61321
email: **helmpress@ktdbroadband.com**

First published 2006

Typeset in Berkley Old Style

ISBN 0 9550823 4 X
978 0 9550823 4 4

Typeset and printed by Stramongate Press, Canal Head, Kendal

Front cover: Ian Ellison, Roger Dangerfield, Derek Marshall, Barry Link
and Roger Downing hauling trek cart over Garburn Pass
as part of their Queen's Scout training.

Back cover: Jim paddling into the sunset

Contents

Jim Cannon

Introduction

I was born in the winter of 1929 to John and Annie Cannon (nee Bracken) when they were farming to the north of Kendal. My father died when I was very young and I moved with my mother, my older brother Ralph and sister Margaret to Lower House in Natland. This remained my home until 1997 when I moved a few hundred metres up the lane

I attended St. George's Primary School and later Heversham Grammar School. When I left school I went to work as an office junior at the Westmorland County Hall in the Education Department until I joined the army, where I reached the rank of sergeant. In 1949 I returned to the Education Department, but left the following year to work in a textile mill at Chorley, owned by Colonel Heaton of Prizet, where I trained to do 'Time and Motion Studies'. This sojourn was to be short, though, as the atmosphere in a textile mill is not the best for a sufferer of asthma! My next job was with the Gas Board where I worked for four years until, in 1955, I went back to the Education Department. In 1974, when the county of Westmorland ceased to exist, if only in the eyes of officialdom, I was lucky enough to land a job with the newly established National Park Authority where I worked as an Administration Officer, until I took early retirement in 1987. This job afforded opportunities for getting out and about in the Lake District and was a wonderful way to end my working life.

In 1953 I became involved with the Scout Movement to which I devoted most of my spare time for the next forty years. This was possible because I had remained single, but in 1991, at the age of 62, I found myself in the cold and snow of the Yukon, courting someone I had known when she, a Dane, had been working as an au pair in Natland thirty odd years earlier! I married Kirsten in the summer of 1992 and brought her to live in the milder climes of Westmorland. When I turned 65, I surrendered my Scout Leader's warrant, but continued to attend the weekly meetings in the capacity of advisor for another five years.

At times I have felt rather sad that, when my contemporaries and I are no longer here, the early history of the 1st Kendal Scout Group would be more or less forgotten, so at the beginning of this year I decided to put pen to paper. My book is not to be viewed as an accurate historical document, but more as personal memories of a nearly fifty-year-long connection with the Group. Memory is a strange thing, however, as I would find out many times in talking with fellow Leaders and former members of the Troop.

Other people remembered events, which I thought I recalled quite clearly, differently; in some cases their recollections were definitely closer to the truth than mine, and I have happily gone with their version.

It would be wrong to say that writing this book has not been hard work at times, but the fringe benefits have been enormous! I have thoroughly enjoyed reminiscing with many of my former Scouts, fellow Leaders in the Group and parents from some of the early years. Ken and Barbara Hughes, who have sadly died since I started the book, Syd Turney, who now lives in New Zealand with his wife Madge and is in his nineties, and Margaret Hall have all contributed their memories

A big thank you goes to Alan Baker, whose memory is second to none, for his considerable contributions to the book, and to two other former Senior Scouts, John Barber and Roger Downing, who told me things that I never knew went on! Thank you also to Terry Howarth and Philip Hutchings, former Leaders, John Atkinson and Ron Starkey, parent volunteers, and others too numerous to mention. Trevor Hughes has been an invaluable help in restoring and organising my old photographs. Jean Scott-Smith kindly transcribed the dialect passages.

The biggest thank-you of all goes to my wife for her support, for all her typing and for making my story more readable and grammatical than I could have managed. (She says that any mistakes in capitalisation are deliberate - for clarification). How humbling it is to find that Kirsten, who was educated in Denmark, has a better grasp of the English language than me (should that be 'I'?)!

I have found it impossible to include all the people who played a part in the life of 1st Kendal, and I am particularly sad not to have been able to get more of the boys' names in. After all, it is they who have made the 1st Kendal the success it is. Without all of them, my life would have been the poorer!

Jim Cannon

Jim Cannon
October 2006

NB If any reader with a connection to the 1st Kendal should have memories to share, I would be delighted to hear from them, although I shall not be writing another book. My telephone number is 01539 722416.
Email address: jkcannon@natland.fsworld.co.uk

Chapter One

A Seed is Sown

Everyone remembers at least one event from 1953. So much happened that year to make it memorable! We all rejoiced when, after a lapse of twenty years, our cricketers achieved the impossible and won back the Ashes. Our young queen, Elizabeth, was crowned with due pomp and ceremony. A fortunate few even enjoyed the spectacle on T.V. At 38, Stanley Matthews won his first cup winners medal in a 4-3 thriller between Blackpool and Bolton Wanderers. In the Himalayas Edmund Hillary and Sherpa Tensing became the first to climb Mount Everest.

I savoured all these happenings from my home village of Natland – a rural idyll just south of Kendal in the old county of Westmorland. In the long ago, Natland had been heaving with activity from its treacle mines. Sadly, all the physical signs of their existence had long gone and they remained only in folklore. Life in Natland in 1953 moved along at an unhurried pace. I was 24. I had a steady job and a special girlfriend of long standing. I owned a D.M.W. trials motorbike and was a paid-up member of the Westmorland Motor Club. What more could a young man want? Life was good and I could not have foreseen that by the end of the year, I would have added 'Scoutmaster' to my C.V.

Most readers will know that the Scout Movement was started by Lord Baden-Powell who had returned home a national hero after his successful defence of the besieged Mafeking during the South African war. When in 1907 his ideas for the formation of a worldwide youth organisation that emphasized character, citizenship and outdoor life were launched, they became an immediate success, quickly spreading throughout the world, even to Westmorland. By 1909 Scout Troops had been established in both Windermere and Kendal.

In the early days of the movement, it was not unusual for the gentry to bestow patronage on a local Troop and the first Scouts in Kendal bore the grand title 1st Kendal (Lady Bagot's Own), the lady in question being Lady Bagot of Levens Hall. It is unclear whether her patronage bestowed benefits on the Troop other than 'status'. This Troop was disbanded in 1939, leaving only the 4th Kendal, under the leadership of Chris Mark, to carry on the good work. Stuart Davidson, well-known for his many years as a player with Kendal Rugby Club, including a spell as its captain, was a member of the

Lady Bagot inspecting 1st Kendal Troop at Leven's Hall, circa 1910.

4th Kendal from 1941 till 1947. He remembers that they met in a large upstairs room above Andrew Brown's Auto Electrician's premises in Wildman Street. Chris Mark's two assistants were Bill Levens and a Mr. Rogerson. Sadly, Mr. Rogerson died in middle age and Stuart recalls helping to convey his coffin in the Troop's trek cart from his home in Vicarage Terrace to the cemetery for burial. A fitting way to go for a Scout Leader!

Stuart remembers his first camp on Potter Fell one bank holiday weekend when the trek cart was also used to transport all their equipment on the three mile journey from Kendal. The Group had an excellent Fife and Drum Band and throughout the war years they played an important part in the civic life of Kendal, leading many a parade through the town. Sid Armstrong who worked at K Shoes was the drum major. Stuart was one of the drummers along with Peter Huddleston, Roy Sarginson, Raymond Wightman, Derek Mark and Bill Sykes as the bass drummer. The fifers included Lesley Leak, Colin Welsh and Jack Holdsworth.

Stuart obtained the King's Scout Badge and in 1946 was selected to take part in the King's Birthday Parade at Windsor Castle. The following year he was chosen to represent Westmorland at the sixth World Jamboree held at Moisson in France. He recalls the thrill of travelling abroad for the first time, and this 'Jamboree of Peace' is remembered for the great heat of that year, the elaborate torchlight opening and the vast arena shows. At the Jamboree, Stuart played Rugby for England against Scotland, but on the day the Scottish team proved too good.

Sadly, in the early fifties, this Troop also disbanded, but was to be reformed a few years later under the leadership of John Major, Kendal's Chief Public Health Officer.

During the few years where no Scout Troop existed in Kendal, Margaret Hall, a secretary at the Provincial Insurance Company, ran a Cub Pack in the Y.M.C.A. in club rooms above what is now McKay's shop near the Town Hall. She had been asked by Derek Webb, then Leader of the Kendal Y.M.C.A., to start the Pack in order to keep the Scout Movement alive in Kendal, and for some time he acted as her assistant.

I occasionally visited the club for a game of snooker, and one evening over a cup of coffee, Derek approached me about the possibility of starting a Scout Troop in the Y.M.C.A. Apart from some of the older Cub Scouts in Margaret's Pack who would soon be ready to move into Scouts, he also had a list of boys in the town who would like to join.

4th Kendal Fife and Drum Band. Drum Major: Sid Armstrong. Fifers: Leslie Leak, Colin Welsh, Jack Holdworth. Drummers: Stuart Davidson, Peter Huddleston, Roy Sargisson, Raymond Wightman, Derek Mark and Bill Sykes (on bass drum).

4

I had grave doubts about taking on this task, and to this day cannot understand why I agreed, but Derek, having already cajoled Margaret into becoming involved in the Movement, must have been a master of persuasion. As I recall, his words went something like this: 'It's only for a couple of hours a week, Jim, and I will do the paperwork for you and help where I can.' Scout Leaders up and down the country will recognize these 'famous last words!'

Although I didn't need Scouts, or any big responsibility, in my life at this time, I did have happy memories of my time as a Scout when I was a boy. In the war years, E. J. Ward, Headteacher at Natland School (1941–45), ran a Troop for the boys of Natland and Oxenholme, including the boys from St. Mark's Home. He was an inspirational leader who provided us boys with wonderful opportunities for adventure and character building. To this day, I often wonder what motivated him, a teacher who spent all day with children, to don short trousers in all weathers, get on his bike carrying a rucksack with all his scouting gear and head off back to Natland school to spend another two hours with a group of boisterous boys!

The war did not constrain my activities, but perhaps rather enhanced them. To me Natland was an exciting place to be, especially after the population grew considerably with the influx of evacuees from Merseyside and the North East. Facilities at the school were soon stretched to the limit. Mr. Cartmel, a respected Natlander, had responsibility for billeting the evacuees. For some obscure reason, he was known to us all as 'Froggy' Cartmel. There was certainly no 'French connection'. He wore a mac and bicycle clips and was seldom seen without his trusty steed. At our house we welcomed an eleven year old boy from Liverpool into the family. I liked him a lot and was sorry when he left because of homesickness.

As in other parts of England, the whole village responded to Churchill's call to unite against the enemy. The women, many of whom had taken on extra work caring for the evacuees, joined the Women's Voluntary Service. Mrs. Keesey, who had lost her husband in W.W.1 and was to lose her only son in W.W.2, was in charge. Their headquarters at St. Mark's Vicarage was a hive of activity with women training to meet with any emergency. I remember on one occasion my mother bringing home a thermos flask she had won in a First Aid competition and another time it was a hot water bottle. Members of the W.V.S. also knitted socks and scarves, gloves and balaclavas and packaged them up to send to the troops overseas. On top of all this, many also responded to the call to 'Dig for Victory' so were more than usually busy growing food. Even the school had a garden where the children could do their bit to help. It was located behind the schoolhouse on part of the land where the village hall now is.

Farmer, Jack Howson from Town End, a tall, erect, imposing figure had been appointed a Special Constable. One of his duties was to go around advising people on how to black out all light from the house and on these visits, he would always be smartly dressed in leather leggings, riding breeches and a tweed jacket. One Saturday night my mother was busy preparing our weekly treat of chips, when there was a loud knock at the door and Mr. Howson's voice boomed: 'Your chimney is on fire, Mrs. Cannon! You'll have to get it out or the Germans will be dropping their bombs on us!' Out came the stirrup pump with which we had been issued so we could put out fires from German incendiary bombs. Its effect on the chip pan fire, however, was minimal and putting out a chimney fire in a 17th century house proved far from easy. In addition to the water, we tried throwing salt up the chimney, but in the end had to wait for the fire to burn itself out, which it did before it was spotted by the enemy.

The Home Guard comprised men between 17 and 65 who were in reserved occupations, many of them young farmers and men waiting to go into the armed forces. The Natland and Oxenholme Platoon of the Home Guard, under the command of Lieutenant Dawson of Castlesteads, used to meet in a back room at the Station Inn and they had a look-out post on Larkrigg Hill. This vantage point afforded views as far away as Arnside, but, because the members of the Home Guard were all working men, it was only manned at night! My brother, who for a short time was a member prior to joining the Royal Navy, tells me that two men would be on duty every night ready to report sightings of enemy aircraft and parachutists, although he does not recall how this reporting was to be done as they had no two-way radio or other communications device. However, we have all watched Dad's Army and know how much can be achieved on bicycle or by shanks's pony.

The actual look-out post was an old Dallam bus which had been dragged up there to provide shelter. I remember that bus very well, mainly because later on in the war, this particular activity by the Home Guard was abandoned, and I got some of the wooden floor boards and used them to make a 'geordie'. Everyone my age will know that this was a wagon made from pram wheels and boards. I remember having two. One was just a flat-boarded one which I used in gathering wood for the fire at home. The other was a super deluxe model and had a car seat mounted on it. When used for riding on, a friend was needed to push you along.

Mr. Ward managed to instil a feeling in us Scouts that we were making a contribution to the war effort. I remember on several occasions being a 'casualty', complete with 'blood' and moans and groans, for the Home Guard to practice their first aid on in their training exercises and having to endure being bandaged up, having splints applied to various limbs and being stretchered to 'safety'. In return, the Home Guard helped us in a small way with our Scout training. One of the proficiency badges many of us tackled was the Cyclist's Badge. In the book 'Boy Scout Tests and How to Pass Them' it states that the Scout 'has to sign a certificate that he owns, or has the use of, and has had the use of for at least 6 months, a bicycle or a motorcycle, in good working order, correctly equipped with lamp, bell or horn, rear reflector or rear lamp and pump, and that he is able and willing to use it in the King's Service if called upon at any time in case of emergency'. Another requirement was to 'repeat correctly a verbal message after a ride of at least one hour's duration'. For this part of the badge, Skip Ward had arranged with the Home Guard for the message to be repeated to the two sentries manning the Larkrigg look-out post. I've forgotten the route I took which must have been a journey of around 10 miles, but I do recall climbing up the hill and the feeling of elation as I made my way home with a note confirming that my message had been accurate. A couple of other war related activities I remember involved the collection of paper and scrap metal and the gathering of rosehips. As far as I know, the purpose in picking these vitamin laden fruits was for use in rosehip syrup to be given to expectant mothers and babies and **not** for itching powder put down the backs of your fellow Scouts! The Troop benefited from the payment of three pence per pound for this work.

Throughout these exciting times we made steady progress with our badge work. Dixon Fox, the owner of Larkrigg Farm, allowed us to camp in a wooded field close to the River Kent, about half a mile from Hawes Bridge. This area gave us plenty of opportunity to practice outdoor skills and pass tests. We cooked on wood fires, we laid tracking signs and followed trails, we swam in the river and learned how to use map and compass and we slept in bivouacs which we made from materials gathered on site. Across from the camp on the site of the old gunpowder works, the army had established an ammunition dump. It was so well screened by dense trees that if we hadn't caught sight of the occasional soldier, we would hardly have known it was there. Colin Milburn, a fellow Natland Scout, remembers one bank holiday camp when a huge storm, complete with thunder and lightning, woke us from our sleep. Tents had to be rearranged and boys moved from the wettest tents to share with drier companions. In the middle of the storm the sky lit up and the ground shook. We assumed it was a particularly bright shaft of lightning, followed by a crack of thunder, and it wasn't till the next day that we learned that lightning, had struck one of the ammunition stores, causing a serious explosion. It was the nearest we got to being blown up during the whole of the war and we didn't know it was happening!

Travel during the war was restricted, so even the main summer camp had to be held fairly close to home. One year, as I recall, we went to Storth. We enjoyed being by the seaside and made the most of the opportunities that it presented. As part of our pioneering training we constructed a rope bridge across a channel on the beach. We used driftwood, and I distinctly remember one of the main supports snapping in two, just as Mr. Ward was demonstrating how safely to cross to the other side! Thankfully he was none the worse for the experience.

Colin also remembers us presenting a mini Gang Show in the village school. It stands out in his mind for two reasons. The first was that he and his brother provided the musical entertainment and played major parts in sketches and the second, that Canon Miller charged the Troop for the rental of the school hall! I have no personal recollection of this show, so I probably didn't shine in any way!

An area where I was rather good was in semaphore, and I can still do it! One of the First Class tests involved sending and receiving a message in semaphore at twenty letters a minute. On the night of the test half of us were sent to the top of Helm (605 ft.) while the rest stayed with Mr. Ward on the village green. Binoculars were needed at both stations and most of us completed the test satisfactorily, although I was reprimanded for having gone right to the top of the hill rather than standing slightly below so the flags would have been more visible!

The Ambulance Badge was probably the most difficult to obtain, but we were fortunate to have the expert tuition of a qualified St. John Ambulance instructor. Joe Allen, who lived at Town End Cottage, worked as an inspector for L.M.S. Railway Company and tutored us over a period of weeks. This culminated in the presentation of the cherished Ambulance Badge to be worn on both arms. How proud I was to wear this very distinctive white badge bearing a red cross!

One thing I did not like about our uniform was the black neckerchief, but Mr. Ward had chosen it because fabric of this colour was cheap and readily available as it was used for black-out curtains! Perhaps he had been influenced by some of the mothers in those austere times?

When Mr. Ward left, I was on the verge of becoming a King's Scout, having completed all the requirements. Unfortunately, my first class hike journal (which I still have) was never sent in as nobody took over the Troop, so to my regret I never did receive that final accolade! However, everything I learned during my years in the 1st Natland Troop was to stand me in good stead in my 42 years as Leader in 1st Kendal.

Scouts attending the first camp in 1954

Campers on the steamer from Lakeside to Bowness. Back row, L/R: Teddy Capstick, David Goff, John Townley, Neil Langhorne and Peter Duckworth; Middle row: Lenny Postlethwaite, Ian Smith and Alan Troughton. Front row: Michael Molloy, Stan Hooton, Brian Little and Roger Tomlinson.

Chapter Two

A Steep Learning Curve

I was aware that my few years as a Scout when I was a boy were hardly adequate training for leading my own Troop, but when I approached the County Commissioner, a jovial man called Joe Cookson, and told him that I had been asked to start up 1st Kendal again and that I could use any advice he could offer, his answer was, 'That's grand, Jim, well done! I'm sure you'll do a great job! Just play some games and teach them some knots and you'll soon get the hang of it!' So with the enthusiasm of youth and armed with a copy of Lord Baden-Powell's 'Scouting for Boys', I followed his advice and got on with it!

In September 1953 I found myself standing in front of fifteen boys raring to go. The ones who came from Cubs arrived in full Cub uniform, the sleeves of their dark green jerseys covered with badges, confirming their achievements in the Pack. Derek Webb had written to the parents of the new boys asking them not to buy uniforms until such time as their boys had completed the Tenderfoot training and were ready to be invested. Yet, as I looked out over the Group, I saw a uniform shirt on one boy, a Scout belt on another and even green garter tabs holding up one boy's stockings. As the crowning glory, one boy wore the broad-brimmed khaki hat with the four dents in it, which Lord Baden-Powell had introduced back in 1907! This would prove a bad investment as the green beret took its place before the year was out.

As the boys called out their names, I noticed certain features about some of them which were to leave a lasting impression. There was a smiling David Goff, who had been a Scout in the disbanded 4th Kendal. With his shorts rolled up and his arms folded across his chest, he seemed keen to get started. Mike Molloy stood out because of his distinctive blue corduroy shorts. In the 1950s school boys didn't get their first long trousers until they were 13 or 14 but, as I remember it, David frequently wore shorts well beyond that age and not just in summer. I imagine the shorts, but not the smile, had gone before he became a maths teacher at schools in Manchester and Chester! Mike's blue cords also became a feature in the Troop as nearly everyone else wore khaki. Five years on, when he gained the Queen's Scout Award, he still wore them, although not the ones he started out with!

By the time he was invested, a boy was expected to have his full uniform consisting of a green beret, khaki shirt, ditto short trousers, a neckerchief fastened at the throat by a woggle and green garters to hold up plain knee stockings. Each Scout Troop is recognisable by the colour of its neckerchief and we opted for red.

With Scout training boys are divided into patrols of six to eight, and an older, experienced and skilled Scout is made Patrol Leader and given responsibility for training 'his' boys. The Scoutmaster's responsibility is to give the P.L. guidance and training on how to do the job. It is an established system that works well. However, because these boys were young and mostly new to Scouting, I had to approach matters differently and for a while I did most of the teaching myself. To this end, I had as previously mentioned, acquired a copy of Baden-Powell's book, 'Scouting for Boys', described as a handbook for good citizenship through woodcraft.

At the first meeting we discussed the Tenderfoot test which they would have to pass before they could be invested. Then, as now, the main requirement was knowledge and understanding of the Scout Law. In 1953 there were ten laws to memorise, against seven today. When you read 'Scouting for Boys', it becomes clear that the law, or perhaps even more the accompanying explanations, had to be modernised. Boys nowadays would be bemused by Scout Law No. 8 '*A Scout smiles and whistles under all difficulties*', and if that isn't enough, the explanation following reads: '*When he gets an order he should obey it cheerily and readily, not in a slow, hang-dog sort of way. Scouts never grouse at hardships, nor whine at each other nor grumble when put out, but go on whistling and smiling. When you miss a train, or someone treads on your favourite corn – not that a Scout ought to have such things as corns – or under any annoying circumstances, you should force yourself to smile at once, and then whistle a tune, and you will be all right. The punishment for swearing or using bad language is for each offence a mug of cold water to be poured down the offender's sleeve by the other Scouts. It was the punishment invented by the old British scout, Captain John Smith three hundred years ago.*' My wife, who comes from a Scouting family in Denmark, tells me that they, as could be expected from descendants of the Vikings, went one step further, giving 'buksevand' as punishment. When I tell you that 'buks' means trouser and 'vand' means water, you can guess the rest!

The Scout Law and the Promise are what makes the Scout Movement unique throughout the world. The original laws were:

A Scout's Honour is to be Trusted.
A Scout is Loyal.
A Scout's Duty is to be Useful and to Help Others.

A Scout is a Friend to All and a Brother to Every Other Scout, no matter to
   what Social Class the Other belongs.
A Scout is Courteous.
A Scout is a Friend to Animals.
A Scout Obeys Orders.
A Scout Smiles and Whistles under all Difficulties.
A Scout is Thrifty.
A Scout is Clean in Thought, Word and Deed.

The modern version, however, is much more relevant to boys of today:

A Scout is to be trusted.
A Scout is loyal.
A Scout is friendly and considerate.
A Scout belongs to the world-wide family of Scouts.
A Scout has courage in all difficulties.
A Scout makes good use of time and is careful of possessions and property.
A Scout has self-respect and respect for others.

These laws have to be memorised and to this end each of the boys, on that
night in 1953, was given a copy to take home. I spent part of each meeting
leading up to the investiture on discussing how both the law and the motto
'Be Prepared' were relevant in their young lives.

The Scout Promise which is made at the point of investiture is important to
every Scout and reaffirmed on occasions such as St. George's Day parades.
It goes as follows:

On my honour,
I promise to do my best
To do my duty to God
And to the Queen,
To help other people
And to keep the Scout Law.

If I had confronted them with all this on the first night, I doubt whether the
boys would have come back the following week, so we played some rousing
games and talked about the fun things we were going to do in the future.
As required, the meeting concluded with prayers. My prayers were always
kept simple and acceptable to Roman Catholics and Protestants of different
denominations alike.

During the first weeks we continued to make steady progress with the

Tenderfoot training. When the weather permitted, we made good use of the open areas in the town, Serpentine Wood, Fletcher Park and Gooseholme in particular. Although Derek Webb kept his word and did the paperwork for the Troop, indeed making himself Group Scoutmaster in the process, it soon became evident that I would need more adult assistance. Quite unexpectedly I arrived one night for a meeting to be greeted by a man with an offer of help. He was Clarry Walker, an affable, unflappable character who oozed good companionship. He was to become a huge support to me and a very close friend. He was in his early thirties, married with a young family and was a printer at the Westmorland Gazette. I never found out what prompted him to come along that night, but his wife, Marjorie, confirms that he had been helping Reg Long, a work colleague at the Gazette, run a Scout Troop at Staveley. I guess that when 1st Kendal started up, he found it more convenient to help with a Troop in the town.

With an extra Leader we made good progress and before Christmas the whole Troop had passed their Tenderfoot test, been invested and had started their training towards gaining their Second Class Badge. One evening we had a surprise visit from our District Commissioner, the Reverend Basil Robinson, Vicar of Skelsmergh. He arrived resplendent in full uniform, topped out with the distinctive wide-brimmed hat. His 'shorts' extended down to overlap his knee stockings and only when he sat down did we catch a glimpse of a sliver of bare flesh. To me he mirror-imaged Baden-Powell and I could easily imagine him in the early days being sent forth as an emissary to spread the Gospel of Scouting! The Basil Robinson way of introducing himself was quite unique. Grabbing a boy by the ribs, he would boom forth as if from the pulpit, 'I'll tell you what your weight is, young man.' His predictions were uncannily accurate. Boys eagerly queued up to experience this holy phenomenon. I doubt whether his ice-breaking ploy would be acceptable today, but at that time it was just good fun and totally innocent. Looking back, I hold fond memories of this rather eccentric, kind man!

Around Easter time, Derek Webb suggested that **we**(!) should have a summer camp. Because of our affiliation with the Y.M.C.A., he thought that a suitable location would be a camping field owned by the Y.M. near their national training centre at Lakeside at the south end of Lake Windermere. Being close to the centre would ensure ready help in the event of an emergency. Derek booked the site and sent off the 'Permission to Camp' form to our District Commissioner. His job was to assess whether Clarry and I were competent to run the camp and, if satisfied, to notify the D.C. in the area where the camp was to take place. During the week our camp would be inspected and a report would be sent back to our District Commissioner in Kendal. This is very good practice and ensures that a certain standard is maintained, but at the time I was blissfully unaware of this procedure and remained in this state till the day the camp inspector showed up.

Having decided the camp would take place in July, there was suddenly some urgency in getting on with teaching the necessary skills. Spring and summer in 1954 were very wet and afforded little opportunity for practicing cooking on open fires, and though we did some indoor cooking, it was hardly good training for the real thing. The boys learned to pitch a tent, to use a hand axe for chopping firewood and to make kitchen gadgets out of wood and sisal, using their newly acquired knotting and lashing skills.

Getting all the equipment together was a logistical nightmare. The cash-strapped Y.M.C.A. was unable to help so it was largely a case of scrounging. I remember borrowing a Black's Nijer tent from the vicar at Troutbeck, whose Troop had sadly disbanded, and a Bell tent stamped 'War Department 1913' from Bert Dixon, a work colleague who lived at Sedgwick. Most of our cooking utensils were sourced from rummage sales and were intended for domestic use. Bakelite handles do not perform well on an open fire! Our hardworking Parents' Committee did, however, provide us with three brand new billy cans and a large frying pan.

Sanitation was always a big issue in the early camps and the boys had to be told what to expect and taught how to prepare urinals and build latrines. According to the handbook, a urinal trench had to be 12 inches wide and 15 inches deep and filled with stones, while the latrine trench had to be considerably deeper. The 'seat' was made from logs and very strong lashings! A hessian screen provided some privacy, but it was never a place to linger longer than absolutely necessary.

A list of personal kit, which each boy was expected to bring, was prepared, discussed with the boys and sent home in ample time. This concluded the boys' involvement in the camp preparations, but we Leaders still had to plan meals, activities and, not least, transport to and from Lakeside. In the fifties Guides and Scouts were often transported in cattle wagons with clean straw on the floor, but we were fortunate to have the services of a Natland builder, Pearson Charnley, who over the years was to do me many a good turn, and Pearson agreed to transport the boys and their equipment in the back of his open builder's lorry. As part of my camp preparation I had read a book called 'The Way to Camp'. In the section dealing with transport it warned

The soggy hay meadow which was the site of my first camp - Lakeside 1954.

that boys travelling in open lorries must remain seated and face backwards. Under no circumstances must they stand up and look over the cab whilst on the move or sore eyes would be the consequence! I actually worried more about this than the possibility of losing one or two boys off the back of the lorry!

When the day finally arrived, it was fine but overcast after a long spell of wet weather. I went ahead on my motorbike, with responsibility weighing more heavily on my shoulders than the rucksack I was carrying. The Scouts' motto is 'Be Prepared', but I was totally unprepared for the sight that confronted me at the campground. I could not believe my eyes! The grass had not been cut and was standing a foot high. There was nothing in my 'Way to Camp' book about haymaking! As I surveyed the soggy mess, I heard movement behind and turned to see an elderly man hobbling slowly towards me, carrying a scythe over his shoulder. He looked for all the world like the grim reaper! As he drew near, he enquired whether I was with the Scouts and on seeing my nod continued, 'It's bin far ower wet te git t'girse cut, hooivver, if thoo sez where thoo's ganna set t'tents, Ah'll set tull reet away.' He quickly completed the task and departed, leaving a few bare patches in a sea of knee-high grass.

When the lorry arrived, the first thing I heard was, 'Skip, Skip, Jonesy (not his real name as I cannot recall who it was) kept standing up and looking over the cab.' At that time my thoughts were too firmly focussed on the job ahead to be concerned about the words of a telltale. I had planned on discussing the lay-out of the campsite with the boys before letting them choose a plot for their patrol tents, but this idea was now scuppered! I allocated the sites and left the boys to get on with pitching their tents. When all the tents were up, Clarry supervised the building of the 'kitchen', while I got busy with a few boys digging the latrines in a nearby wood. Boys who were not involved in these jobs were employed making gadgets and collecting firewood.

Except for one boy, Peter Duckworth, who was older than the rest and had come to us from 4th Kendal, the boys – and we Leaders too, for that matter - were all inexperienced campers. Because of this and because our equipment was inadequate, we had decided to abandon the Patrol system and cook for the whole Troop on one fire with individual Patrols taking turns helping. I was to rue this decision, as meal preparation ended up taking an inordinate amount of time. Of course, I knew that the Patrol system was fundamental to the Movement, but in this case I must have thought I knew better. Several years later during formal Scouters' training I wrote in my notes, 'Failure to use the Patrol system results in failure!' Hindsight is indeed a wonderful thing! The awful weather didn't help either! I remember that one day torrential rain actually put out the fire! In those conditions I think even Ray Mears would have struggled.

Fortified by a substantial breakfast the boys lined up for their first morning inspection. During this daily routine, I would make sure that the boys were clean and happy and that the campsite was tidy. When I got to 'Jonesy', I immediately noticed his red eyes. Surprise, surprise! The book had been right and I should have made sure my First Aid kit contained the proper medication to deal with the problem! Miraculously, the small village shop at Finsthwaite, sadly no longer there, stocked 'Golden Eye Ointment', but whereas a pharmacist might have warned me that the condition might be infectious, the postmaster at Finsthwaite did not, and consequently I ended up with sore, red eyes myself!

I suppose it is not surprising that, at the age of 24, I worried a great deal about the health of the boys before taking them to camp. I distinctly remember reading in Baden-Powell's 'Scouting for Boys' about the importance of keeping your bowels regular and advice on how to achieve this. Looking back at it now, his health advice is rather dated. In Camp Fire Yarn No. 18 under HEALTH-GIVING HABITS it reads:

*(And) to be healthy and strong, you **must** keep your blood healthy and clean inside you. This is done by breathing in lots of pure, fresh air, by deep breathing, and by clearing out all dirty matter from inside your stomach, which is best done by having a movement daily without fail; many people are better for having it twice a day. If there is any difficulty about it one day, drink plenty of good water, especially before and just after breakfast, and practise body-twisting exercises, and all should be well. Never start to work in the morning without some sort of food inside you.*

Little did I know that by the middle of the week I would be the one in need of relief! I do not recall if it was because we didn't have enough 'good water' or because I had learned elsewhere of the benefits of orange juice, but off I went in search of some Britvic Orange. I found it in the Lakeside Hotel, bought six bottles, immediately downed two and followed them up with two more before I went to bed. In case you are wondering, yes, it does work and no, a camp latrine is not a pleasant place to linger, particularly in the middle of the night!

We had planned a full programme before leaving home, but the poor weather forced us to make many changes. However, we did manage to do some of the planned activities. We hiked to the High Dam, splashed around briefly in the cold lake, played lots of games and worked with map and compass. Looking back, though, it seems as if we spent most of our time collecting wood for the fire, cooking and washing up. Perhaps that is why one special day stands out in my memory.

It was in the middle of the week. After yet another late lunch, Clarry generously suggested that I take the boys off to Bowness on the lake steamer. He would do all the washing up. What an offer! In no time at all the boys and I, spruced up and fully uniformed, were heading for the pier. As we set sail, the sun shone and I was soon fast asleep, leaving the boys to explore the boat and spend some of their pocket money. In Bowness the boys were given free time while I enjoyed a cup of non-smoky tea in a café. Sitting in this civilised environment, warm and dry, I thought with gratitude of Clarry, slaving away to bring some order back to the camp before our return. Little did I know that he'd had a more exciting afternoon than us!

It was a happy band of boys who returned to the camp. We could even have been 'smiling and whistling'! Seeing the tidy camp kitchen, I asked Clarry how he had got on. 'Don't ask,' he said, 'you wouldn't believe what happened. After you lot left, I was lying on me bed having a fag waiting for the water to get hot when I heard this posh voice calling 'Hello, anybody there?' and when I stuck me head out of the tent, there was this tall figure wearing a white riding mac and a Baden-Powell Scout hat. Guess who it was? The bleeding District Commissioner come to do the camp inspection! I told him where you'd gone and then he asked to see the camp. He started at the kitchen. Disaster! I hadn't even started cleaning up. He then methodically worked his way around from tent to tent picking up bits of litter on the way. When he went into the wood to see the toilets, he found a branch chopped off a tree. He was not impressed! I didn't offer him a cup of tea, but I don't think he would have wanted to stay for one anyway.'

I was very relieved when, on the Saturday, Pearson Charnley arrived in his lorry to take us home! It had been a long week! I hope the boys got something positive out of the camp and learned from the experience. I know I did!

Two weeks later I bumped into Basil Robinson in town. He greeted me cheerily, 'Oh, Jim, I have had the report on your camp. I don't think I am going to give it to you, but I am sure you will do better next time.' What an understanding man!

1st Kendal Scout Group assembled in Fletcher Park, 1960. The Leaders (left to right): Ken Hughes, David Bone, Terry Howarth, Clarry Walker, Jim Cannon, Syd Turney, Margaret Hall, Barbara Hughes, Madge Turney and Nancy Dangerfield.
Courtesy Westmorland Gazette Photo

Chapter Three

From Small Beginnings

There was no shortage of boys wanting to join when Margaret Hall started her Cub Pack back in the early fifties. When she moved to Kendal, she was already a fully trained Leader with experience of running a Pack in the South East. In the early days her weekly support came from Derek Webb and two young employees of the North Western Gas Board. Eric Hunt worked in the accounts department and Roy Mottram was the distribution engineer for Kendal and the Lakes. He was also my boss during the four years that I worked for the Board. Roy found himself roped in to help because his wife was a work colleague of Margaret's. Stories about the way people were recruited as Scout Leaders could fill a book.

Roy's position with the Board entitled him to a Ford Consul or an Austin A40, but for some unknown reason he was unable to obtain a driver's licence and I recall that his 'company vehicle' was an L-plated B.S.A. Bantam motorbike. Somehow this basic transport never seemed to affect his cheery disposition, even on wet days.

Aside from Eric and Roy, I believe almost all of Margaret's friends found themselves helping out for longer or shorter periods and for weekend activities there were always sufficient parent volunteers.

Alec Duff, a factory manager at K Shoes, and his wife, Marion, whose sons Bill and Jim were in the Pack, were stalwart helpers for many years as their boys progressed from Cubs through to Senior Scouts. In the 1930s the K Shoe Company established a fellwalking base for its employees at Seathwaite in Borrowdale. Alec was able to pull strings and make it possible for the Cubs and later for the Scouts to make use of these facilities on many weekends. Margaret recalls Alec and Bryan Stilling, who also worked at K's, taking the Cubs on hikes from the hostel and teaching them simple map reading and how to use a compass. Serious walks were undertaken including journeys to the summits of Great Gable and Scafell! Not many people today can boast that they climbed to the top of England's highest mountain when they were still under eleven years old. Many readers familiar with Bryan Stilling's good work with both the Langdale and Ambleside Mountain Rescue Team and the Lake District Voluntary Warden Service will know that the boys were in safe hands.

As the Cub Pack flourished so did the fledgling Scout Troop and when the Gas Board came up with yet another Leader, this time for the Scouts, Clarry and I were more than happy. Philip Hutchings, a Sedbergh lad who had been a Scout at Queen Elizabeth School, Kirkby Lonsdale, worked for the Board as a technician in their Kendal laboratory. Right from the start his help with both the weekly meetings and a variety of weekend activities gave the Troop a welcome boost and when he willingly relieved me of responsibility for leading the Troop on civic parades, I couldn't believe my luck. It was a job that I really hated. The Remembrance Day Parade in particular was an ordeal for us Scouts. From memory, this sombre occasion always coincided with the coldest most inhospitable weather of the month. Well before the 11 a.m. two minutes silence, soldiers of the Border Regiment would form up on the Market Place parade ground, snug inside warm battledress and protected by thick army greatcoats. They would soon be joined by sensibly uniformed Sea, Army and Air Cadets. Around this time we Scouts would abandon our 'Be Prepared' motto and join the gathering wearing short trousers and short sleeved shirts. This behaviour could be compared with Noel Coward's sentiment on 'mad dogs and Englishmen'- only the season is different. We frequently courted hyperthermia, and I recall on one occasion having to brave snow flurries. On that morning we took shelter under the awnings of the shops in the Shambles and joined the parade only at the very last moment. At the end of each parade we would hurry to the Y.M.C.A. to thaw out over a mug of hot Vimto. It would be 1967, following a long overdue review of the Scout Movement in the United Kingdom, before long trousers became part of the regulation uniform. My respite from parades was to be short lived when, after two years, Philip left to do his National Service in the R.A.F., and although he briefly returned to Kendal, there was no longer enough excitement for him here and he left to seek his fortune with Colin Chapman at the Lotus Car Company at Cheshunt. That spelt the end of his involvement with 1st Kendal, but not of our friendship. I was his best man when he married Margaret, a Guide Leader, in 1961, am godfather to one of his three sons, and we are still friends to this day. Lotus didn't bring fame and fortune, but Philip had a very good career as finance director with the 'Lincolnshire Echo'.

When I say that Philip's connection with 1st Kendal ended when he left the town, it is not strictly true. Several years later, in 1964, Terry and I were returning from a camping trip to Spain with eight Senior Scouts in the back of a motor caravan. We crossed the Channel late at night, and it soon became clear to me that I could not continue the journey to Kendal without some sleep. Around midnight we descended on Philip and Margaret at their home in Hertford just as they were going to bed. Without hesitation they invited us in, gave Terry and myself beds to sleep in and allowed the boys to spread out their sleeping bags on the lounge floor. The next morning Mark, the very young son of the house, kept calling out – again and again – 'Dad, there is a man coming upstairs!' An early morning photo call caused great interest among neighbours who must have wondered what kind of friends Philip and Margaret had. (see p.134)

When the Government nationalised the electricity industry in 1948, more than forty companies supplying an area stretching from the Scottish border to South Westmorland amalgamated to become the North Western Electricity Board. During the next decade many employees were required to relocate to Kendal where the Board had established its headquarters. Not only did the town's economy benefit from these people coming in and buying homes in the area, but 1st Kendal also made a significant gain by acquiring a fully trained and experienced Leader, David Bone, and an excellent parent volunteer, George Barker.

One night, when I arrived for the weekly meeting, I was met by George who was seeking a place for his son Alan in the Troop. After working briefly for G.E.C. in London at the beginning of the war, he had been transferred by the company to work in West Cumberland and now found himself relocated to Kendal with his wife, Beth, and three children to work at Norweb's new headquarters. I discovered that he was a qualified first-aider with the Board, and when he offered his services in this capacity to the Troop, Alan's membership of the 1st Kendal was assured. Over the years George helped numerous boys gain their qualifications in First Aid. In addition, he was also an invaluable helper with anything practical, such as digging out the foundations of the new headquarters, and he and Beth played a full part in the activities of the Parents' Committee, working tirelessly to raise money for the Group.

At that first meeting George mentioned that he had a work colleague who had been a Scout Leader in Carlisle and who might be interested in joining the 1st Kendal if help was needed. David Bone duly arrived at the next meeting, in full uniform. He spoke in a quiet voice and without wasting any words. I explained briefly the programme for the evening and suggested that perhaps he might like to observe how we did things, but, when he quickly became involved in helping to run the activities, it became obvious that he would be an asset to the Troop. At the end of the meeting I wanted to have a word with him, but he had disappeared, only to turn up again the

Parent helpers Alec and Marion Duff with Margaret Hall at Tarn Hows.

George Barker teaching First Aid to the Scouts.

following week. The same thing happened at the end of that meeting, but the third week I managed to stop him before he left to ask how he felt about joining the Group. He drew a deep breath and paused at length before finally saying, 'Yes, I guess you are good enough.' This was my first encounter with his typical, dry humour.

The next Leader to come on board, in 1958, was Terry Howarth who remains a friend till this day. Terry was an ebullient, easy-going young man with a penchant for big cars and good food. In a relatively short period of time he owned an Austin Atlantic, a Zephyr Zodiac, a 2.4 Jaguar like the one Inspector Morse drove and a Triumph Stag Convertible. I vividly recall that the first time I travelled in a car at 100 mph was in the Zodiac one Sunday evening on the way to Morecambe. Quite an experience for someone used to driving a Ford Anglia with a top speed of about 80 mph with a good tail wind! Skills gained while working as a trainee with the Westmorland Gazette enabled Terry to start a small printing business, working from home. Three years later T. Howarth Printers was established in the former Toc H rooms in Stramongate. Over the years, with lucrative contracts from some of the bigger companies in the town, the business prospered and after 25 years he sold out to his former employees and retired. The business became known as Stramongate Press, the printer of this book. Terry lives with his wife Ann and son Marcus in Grange.

With two extra Leaders helping to run the Troop, Clarry and I were able to start a Senior Scout Group (fifteen and a half to eighteen years). David and Terry ran the Scout Troop for the next two years until numbers dictated that a second Troop was started. At this point Terry became Leader of the A Troop, assisted by one of my former Senior Scouts, John Barber, and David of the B Troop with me as his assistant. John Barber was another employee of the Westmorland Gazette where he trained to be a bookbinder. He later went to work for Terry in his printing business, before setting up Piggery Press, a business he has only recently sold.

Big changes happened in 1959. Margaret Hall's Pack had a long waiting list so when the mother of Trevor Hughes, one of her Cubs, offered to run a second Pack, she was welcomed with open arms. Barbara Hughes, nee Sedgwick – a connection she was always proud of, was born in 1924 and at the age of eighteen she found herself part of a 1,500 strong workforce building Flying Boats at a factory which had been quickly constructed at White Cross Bay near Troutbeck Bridge. Incidentally, prefab houses for the workers and a school for their children had sprung up at the same time at nearby Calgarth, where the Lakes School now stands. With the war over,

The Grand Howl. Margaret Hall with the Rural Pack

Barbara went to work for Jaeger, spending some time at their main shop in London, before returning to Kendal to work at the head office of the Provincial Insurance Company. It was here that she met Ken Hughes whom she married in 1947. Many readers will remember her working at Musgrove's, now Beale's and in her father's butcher shop in the Market Place. (Her father was known not only for his good meat, but also for having an artificial hand). It was here that Barbara gained her knowledge of meat and many of her culinary skills, and over the years many Cubs and Scouts profited from this.

Ken had the unique distinction of being born in Paradise. His earthly Paradise happens to be two rows of cottages located at Ireleth near Askham-in-Furness. His boyhood years were happily spent in a cottage at Broughton Tower where his father worked as a gardener, his mother as a cook. Ken enjoyed being a Scout and also singing in the church choir and till the end of his days knew many of the old hymns by heart. He did well at Ulverston Grammar School and in 1937 found work with the Provincial Insurance Company, where he would spend his entire working life. When war broke out, he volunteered to serve in the Border Regiment and was soon in the thick of things in France and in North Africa. Only toward the end of his life did he volunteer information about his war years, but he was firmly convinced of the futility of war as a means of solving differences between countries.

One of the many roles Ken will be remembered for is that of Leader of a very unique Scout Troop. After the war there were few villages in South Westmorland with enough boys to form a Cub Pack. Rural bus services were poor and, with only a few families owning a car, joining a Pack in Kendal was impractical. Margaret Hall, however, wearing her newly acquired Commissioner's hat, hit on an idea that instead of bringing Cubs to the Pack, she would take the Pack to the Cubs! To make it possible, she sought the help of Women's Institutes and Parish Councils to find a responsible adult in each village, who, after training, would be prepared to run weekly meetings for up to eight boys. In a very short time she had recruited Joe and Frances Carruthers at Burneside, Chris Law at Staveley, Jean Hayhurst at Endmoor, and Grace Robinson and Muriel Nelson at Old Hutton.

On one Saturday afternoon each month, Cubs from all four villages would converge on 1st Kendal's headquarters to enjoy a joint meeting under the leadership of Margaret Hall and Ken Hughes. Kendal and District Rural Cub

Pack was born! Soon Ken took out a Cub Leaders warrant, and when Margaret left, he ran the Pack with the help of Barbara. The parental support for these Cubs was outstanding and the Pack flourished. As the boys reached the age of 10½ they moved on to become Rural Scouts. For many activities, including summer camps, they joined with Scouts from the 1st Kendal, eventually, in 1967, becoming part of the Troop. It was a happy union.

Ken and Barbara continued as Leaders until their retirement in 1984 and even then, they stayed active within the Movement. Ken took on the job of coordinating all the Camp Advisers in the area. (You will notice that the dreaded Camp Inspector of my first camp had now become a Camp Adviser! So much friendlier, don't you think?) Ken personally, more often than not accompanied by Barbara, visited 845 camps and clocked up 15,978 miles in the process! He finally gave up the job in 1996 when he was 75.

Barbara and Ken became close personal friends to me and later to my wife and they were both keen on contributing their memories to this book. Sadly, neither of them lived to see its completion as both passed away this year (2006), Barbara in April and Ken in July.

On the 28th of May 1959 Barbara ran her first Cub meeting, helped by Ken and by Sandra Lansom, a fifteen year old high school girl from Burneside. This Pack ran for seven years, and at different times Barbara was assisted by her sister, Maude Dangerfield, Brenda MacGregor (a secretary at K Shoes), Bea Bone (wife of David) and Pam Ormandy (mother of one of the Cubs). When the need for two Packs was no longer there, Barbara became Akela of the only Pack, which she ran until her retirement. Sandra continued to help Barbara until her marriage in 1967 to Brian Elshaw, one of my Senior Scouts, with whom she left to live in Grizedale Forest. By the time her son Craig was old enough to join the Cubs, she had returned to the area and took up her old post as Assistant Cub Leader. When Barbara retired, Sandra stayed with the Pack assisting the new Akela, Ashley Henderson, who had been one of Barbara's Cubs. Sandra will be remembered for helping out in all sorts of ways, often behind the scenes – decorating, making curtains, arranging a Pony Gymkhana to raise funds for the new hut etc.

Another of Barbara's helpers was a young Queen's Guide by the name of Janet Laycock. Janet married Barbara's son, Trevor, and continued to help with the Cubs until she was expecting her first child, Karen. This, very handily, coincided with Sandra's return to Kendal, so continuation was assured. While Karen was still in school, she became a helper in the Pack, a job she is still doing to this day, and Ashley is still the Cub Scout Leader. Interestingly, Ashley's grandfather had been a Scout and Scoutmaster in the 1st Kendal (Lady Bagot's Own).

In 1960 Margaret left to become Assistant County Commissioner for Cubs in Westmorland. In 1964 Len Reynolds, County Secretary for Scouts and popular Headteacher at Kendal Grammar School, was chosen to serve on the Chief Scout's Advance Party, a national body set up to review all aspects of the Movement and he chose Margaret to be his secretary. Only twenty-four people were selected, so to have one from Westmorland was quite an honour! This body worked tirelessly from January 1964 to June 1966 giving of their own time, examining all aspects of Scouting and studying methods used in other countries. When eventually their recommendations for the future were published, the different committees had met on one hundred and sixty-six occasions and the full working party had met on seven full weekends. It was a huge and important task. In 1965 Margaret left Kendal to take up a post as secretary to the Head of Eton College.

When in 1959 Margaret resigned as Pack Leader, the role of Akela was taken over by Mary Ohlson who hailed from Stockport. Mary had spent some of the war years with her aunt and uncle, Margaret and Johnny Dodgson, at their Natland farm. In the late fifties she had returned to Kendal to work for Westmorland County Council in the Children's Department. Her composed manner and soft voice coupled with a great sense of humour (an essential for any Leader) made her popular with the boys, and A Pack continued to thrive.

Mary's assistant was Michael Sagar, a larger-than-life character, who had been a Cub, Scout and Senior Scout in the 1st Kendal. His enthusiasm in everything he did made him popular with the boys, and his performances in the Gang Shows, which we ran for many years, still bring a smile to my face. Mike married Pat Riding, who had been a Leader with the Pack, and when he died at a very early age from a heart attack, we were all shocked and saddened. A few years later we were numbed by the news that Pat had died from M.S. A sad end to two fine young lives!

When Mary Ohlson returned to Stockport in 1962, leadership of the A Pack was taken over by Sheila Scott who had been her assistant for a short time. Sheila, the only daughter of Mr. and Mrs. John Scott who farmed at Burneside, grew up with six brothers and knew a lot about the peculiar ways of boys. I imagine that running a two hour meeting for 24 boys each week

Westmorland Scouts at 1929 World Jamboree at Arrowe Park, Birkenhead

would have presented her with few problems. In the minutes of the Leaders' meeting held in March 1963, it reads, 'Sheila braved the wettest day of the winter on her scooter and visited Bark House near Ashness Bridge at Watendlath. All she got for her efforts was a thorough soaking. The camp is not suitable for Cubs. A Pack have settled for Tarn Hows.' It was typical of Sheila's determination to get things right. Sheila left in 1966 to marry Peter Hadwin, who was later to become the first full time organiser for Cumbria Young Farmers.

By 1960 the Group had mushroomed to a membership of over one hundred. It was a high point in the history of 1st Kendal and with so much taking place, the need for the Leaders to meet regularly under a strong Group Scout Leader became vital. Issues such as the shared use of our limited resources, particularly our camping equipment, made it important that we were always aware of each other's plans. Our aspirations to have our own headquarters called for a united effort with fund raising and it was a great relief when Syd Turney agreed to take on the job of holding it all together. Syd continued in this role for eight years, and in all this time monthly meetings of all the Section Leaders continued to be held. At the beginning we would enjoy his and his wife Madge's hospitality, with Madge always serving tea and delicious home baking, something we missed when the meetings were switched to our new H.Q. While Syd was G.S.L., meticulous records were kept and these have served to jog my memory during the writing of this book.

Like Ken Hughes, Syd had attended Ulverston Grammar School and also been a Scout. Being five years older than Ken, he had enjoyed the experience of attending the 'Coming of Age World Jamboree' at Arrowe Park in 1929. The two young men met up when they were working at the Provincial, and they both joined the army in 1940. Their wartime experiences, however, were to be very different. Whereas Ken was to see action on foreign soil, Syd describes himself as 'the soldier who never was'. Syd's war years were spent training and re-training for a variety of jobs and his army C.V. includes: expert at building Bailey girder and floating pontoon bridges, company pay clerk, mine explosives expert, a member of the Royal Engineers' sabotage unit, commissioned in the Royal Artillery and qualified glider pilot through the R.A.F. Like most soldiers, Syd wanted to go and confront the enemy, but his one and only foray into enemy territory was to be of short duration. His arrival in France coincided with the army's defeat at Dunkirk and within days he found himself back at San Malo docks, just in time to catch the last ferry to leave France for a very long time. He must have been relieved to have come through the war without firing a rifle, an artillery piece or an explosive at the enemy!

While training to become an officer, Syd met Madge who was a member of the A.T.S. (Auxilliary Territorial Service). Madge had been trained to drive and maintain any type of vehicle from American Jeeps and staff cars, to Bren gun carriers and armoured cars. She hated these because the driver's vision through an oblong visor to the front and one to the side was so restricted, that she had to rely on the eyesight and skill of an observer standing with her head out of the turret! Syd and Madge were married in 1944 and it was the birth of their daughter Elizabeth that finally enabled Madge to leave the Services.

When Syd retired in about 1971, he and Madge moved to New Zealand to be near Kevin, their son, who had emigrated there earlier, leaving the now married Elizabeth behind. In 1992 they returned to the Kendal area and our friendship was renewed. Syd, however, could not get used to the cold and rather damp climate of Westmorland so after eight years, and at the age of 85, he announced that they were returning to the more comfortable lifestyle of the Southern Hemisphere!

One of the greatest rewards a Scout Leader can have is to see some of his former Scouts go on to become Leaders. Alan Baker ran Scouts in Cartmel and Roger Downing ran a Troop in Swansea for many years before returning to Kendal in 1993, when he became Leader of the 1st Kendal Scout Troop. Some, such as Trevor Hughes and Geoff Bainbridge, never left the Group, but went on through the system, finally becoming Scout Leader and Venture Scout Leader, respectively. Chris Head, who was in my Troop in the 1970s, is another 1st Kendal 'graduate' who has stayed with the Group. He is still an Assistant Scout Leader with special responsibility for the Troop finances.

In 1967 Tim Keegan, a graduate trainee with K Shoes, joined the Group as an Assistant Scout Leader. Two years later, to the great relief of Syd Turney, he took over as Group Scout Leader. Tim is involved in a number of voluntary organisations in Kendal and 1st Kendal continues to benefit from his organisational skills nearly forty years on.

Tim's arrival was only one of many significant events in the Group's history in 1967. Clarry retired from Scouting and Terry left to run his business. Until a District Venture Scout Unit was formed, I continued running the Senior Scout Section with only a handful of boys and alongside this, I was also Assistant Scoutmaster. Having only one Cub Pack caused a knock-on effect so at this point there was also only one Troop. David Bone was the Leader until he decided he wanted less responsibility and in 1969, with him as my assistant, I took over running the Troop again.

Reunion of early 1st Kendal Leaders 1991. L/R Ken Hughes, Sheila Hadwin (Scott), Barbara Hughes, Jim Cannon, Madge Turney, Terry Howarth, Mary Ohlson and Syd Turney

Chapter Four

The Weekly Meeting

The weekly meeting for both Cubs and Scouts is the life-blood of the Movement, the means for building a successful Troop or Pack and the vehicle for all our training. Planning and running these meetings is a time consuming task and it calls for mental dexterity to come up with a regular supply of new things to do, but woe betide the Leader who tries to throw a meeting together in the last minute. Twenty-four to thirty-six boys do not sit quietly waiting for the leader to think up what to do next.

A Cub Pack ideally consists of twenty-four boys divided into four 'Sixes' each led by a Sixer and a Second, who are responsible for keeping their Six in order. A Scout Troop is divided into Patrols of six or eight boys, each with a Patrol Leader (P.L.) and an Assistant Patrol Leader. The P.L. is responsible for the basic training of the new boys and for the general demeanour and behaviour of his Patrol. To explain how a Cub Pack should be run I have decided to quote an article written by Ken Hughes in 'The Little Aynam News' in April 1970. At that time Ken, with his wife Barbara, had been running the B Pack for eleven years and I can think of no person better qualified to give this explanation than Ken, as he had been working with the best. Barbara was the best planner and most organised Leader I have ever come across. She had weekly planning meetings at her home with all Leaders and helpers to ensure that everyone knew what they had to do at the Pack meeting, what they needed to prepare or perhaps buy. In all Cub Packs worldwide the Leaders take their names from Kipling's Jungle Book with the Scouter in charge, male or female, always being Akela, while others might be Baloo or Raksha. This tradition applies only to the Cubs. All Scout Leaders are addressed as Skip, i.e. Skip Cannon, Skip Howarth etc.

Cub Pack Meeting
(A few notes especially for Cub Scout parents)

We are sure some of you must wonder what happens on Thursday evenings at our weekly Cub meetings. As parents we know that children do not generally provide this information for those at home. In these notes we will try to give an overall picture of the things we do and why we do them.

The official starting time for the meeting is 6.30 p.m. but the boys start to arrive from about 6 p.m. onwards. We like everyone to be present a few minutes before

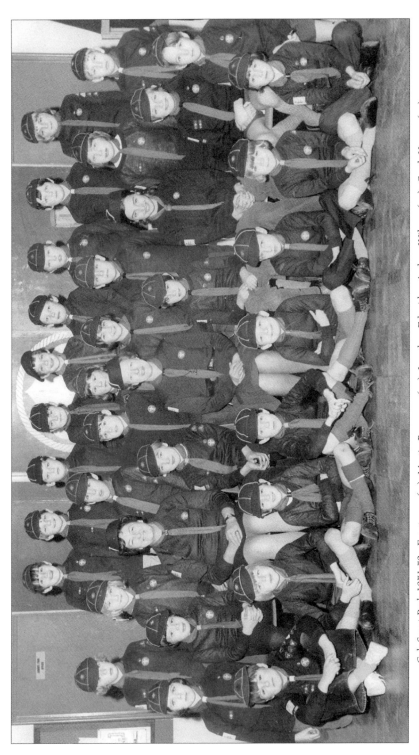

Cub Scout Pack 1971-72. Front row: (..), Martin Rogerson, (…), Jonathan Etheridge, Andrew Wilson, (…), Garth Hamer, (…);
2nd row: Nicholas Dean, David Elwood, Hilda Hayton, Alan Thompson, Barbara Hughes, (…), Janet Laycock, Malcolm Wrigley, Rodney Carradus
3rd row: Philip Talbot, Steve Head, Simon Horsley, (…), Brian Stevenson, David Lecore, (…), Andre Marshall, Ian Stanley. 4th row: Philip Proctor, (…), Graham
Starkey, Simon Just, Mark Lowther, David (?) Retallick, Angus Flockhart, Mark Plenderleith and Mark Pattinson.

Courtesy Westmorland Gazette

6.30 p.m. so that the Sixers can have a final check round for tidiness etc. before the meeting gets underway.

Akela invariably arrives at the H.Q. at 6 p.m. and without fail one or two young men are already waiting to get in (whatever the weather). Many years ago when Akela was less experienced in the ways of Cub Scouts she used to try and arrive a little earlier so that the boys would not have to wait outside. It didn't work, however, because the boys also came a little earlier. She now accepts the inevitable, and – confidentially – would miss these early, smiling lads if they changed their timetable.

During the half hour from 6 to 6.30 p.m. the Leaders are occupied in giving attention to individual requests. Boys hand over their collections, models, reports, plants and many other items we need to see in connection with their progressive Cub Scout tests. As you will know, a fair amount of work for tests is done at home and we are grateful for the co-operation we receive from parents. We never cease to be impressed by the standard achieved by some of the boys but, in our view, what really matters is the amount of effort put into the test. Not everyone will achieve the same standard, but the end result is not of itself the most important thing. It's what happens along the way that really matters. All our tests have been carefully designed not only to provide high objectives but also to point the way to the many interesting and enjoyable paths which can be followed. We do not favour a boy rushing madly at top speed through all his arrow tests – he is likely to miss much of interest on the way – steady progress within his age group is generally best.

We try to keep all the boys moving forward, but with a Pack as large as ours [at one time B Pack had 36 members] we may perhaps overlook a quiet individual. If this happens to be your son, please tell him to grab Akela at the next Pack Meeting and not let go until his problem has been sorted out.

6.30 p. m. (or 18.30 hours to the well-informed)

Grand Howl – This traditional opening gets us off to a good start. The Cubs, standing in a circle, with loud voices affirm that at all times they intend to 'do their best'. (Who could ask for anything more?)

Flag Break – A chosen Sixer or Second breaks the flag. (He has previously folded it and says a silent prayer that it will unfurl when he pulls the rope)!

Inspection - It is good that boys should be clean and tidy. Each Six is inspected in turn and points are awarded. (These Points go towards the monthly total for the 'best' Six). We award weekly pennants for (1) Tidy (2) Clean (3) Alert and (4) 99% Special. These pennants are retained by the Six for the meeting only. 99% Special is awarded on rare occasions when a Six manages to win all the other three pennants. This inspection lark is quite formal but it gives the Leaders a chance to talk to every boy in the Pack. We can also see how the badge work is going from a visual inspection.

We know that you send them off to 'Cubs' like shining new pins but unfortunately things tend to happen on the way to H.Q. and also in the interval before the meeting starts. A roll on the floor is not conducive to a dustless jersey, but it's surprising what a last minute dust-off by the Sixer can achieve. (Comment by one young man last week – 'I always keep my cap in my hand before the meeting. It can't then be used as a football!).

Notices – Chiefly concerns things such as next football fixture – progress of tests – awards of badges – coffee mornings – well done, John Snookes for saving life of pet parrot - etc. etc. (N.B. If it concerns something you really must know about, we try to send you a note – always hoping that it will be removed from the pocket when your son arrives home). By this time the gathering is getting a little restless and is more than ready for a …

Rousing Game – It is remarkable how many variations are possible of basic themes – we try to avoid repeat games unless they are called for by popular request – there are still some good 'old faithfuls' that have been going on for donkey's years. This gets rid of surplus energy so hereafter we can concentrate on various kinds of instruction.

First Aid – At the moment Raksha (Mrs. Hilda Hayton) is nearing completion of a First Aid course for some of the older boys. They break off from the main meeting and have detailed instruction in the office. This is a most important aspect of any Scout training.

Main Programme – The main part of the meeting is a mixture of games, general instruction of the whole Pack or, alternatively, the Sixes working apart on different projects. The Leaders meet the previous evening to work out their plan of action because it is important that there should be no hold-ups whilst we decide what to tackle next.

Enjoyment – Probably the most important aspect of any Cub meeting is that the boys should enjoy themselves and to judge by the noise level this usually happens.

Subject to certain disciplines they can entertain and instruct each other. Lately we have all enjoyed one or two demonstrations of card tricks, coupled with the odd scientific experiment. Play acting is immensely popular, especially when we dress up for the parts.

Too soon – Our finishing time draws near (8 p.m.) and we slip in a fairly quiet session to lower the excitement level before turning them loose for their homeward journey. (If we didn't plan this, they would charge forth like a Pack of wild men on the war path)!!

Grand Howl – Traditional reminder of Cub Scout Promise is followed by the lowering of the Union Flag.

Prayers – We close all our meetings with prayers. The boys stand in a circle with caps off and think about their duty to God. For some time now Mrs. Hayton has been providing the prayers and these are specially thought out so that they are appropriate to the particular meeting. We thought you might like to read our Easter prayer and we therefore set it out below. 'O, Lord, let Thy love shine on these Thy children and as we close our meetings for the Easter holidays, grant that each boy may go out willingly to do his service in Scout Job Week. Grant that their requests for work may fall on sympathetic ears and that they carry out all jobs cheerfully and willingly knowing that in giving service for our Group we also serve Thee, the Greatest Master of All. Help us to remember the supreme sacrifice which was made for us at Easter time and be thankful. Amen.'

The Scout Troop Meeting

For the same edition of 'Little Aynam News' I was asked to tell about a typical Troop meeting. Except for allowances paid to the more advanced ages of the boys – ten and a half to fifteen – a Troop meeting is very similar to a Pack meeting. The meeting I chose to describe took place at the beginning of April 1970:

Another Troop Meeting, 'The Toffee Boilers'

Contrary to popular belief the weekly Troop meeting, as far as the Leaders is concerned, starts not at 7 p.m., but at 5.30 p.m. At this hour, when the taxman loses interest in your toil, the preparation for the 'ordeal' begins. In these ninety minutes you have somehow to fit in commuting, tea bolting, shoe cleaning, equipment gathering, loin girding, indigestion tablet taking and shopping. (We are doing toffee making tonight and yes, I should have got the ingredients earlier).

Pack Colour Party: Bill Duff, Alan Baker and Bruce Cowperthwaite, who eight years later went on to become Queen's Scouts.

Campfire with 1st Kendal Y.W.C.A. Guides.

Back at the H.Q. around 6.30 p.m. half a dozen eager characters are waiting, ready to pile in the moment Skip turns the key. By the time the office is reached, a game of soccer is in progress.

The other Scouters arrive and the evening's programme is explained on the basis of who does what, where and when. At 6.55 p.m. the countdown is started by Skip Bone who announces to the teeming mass 'five minutes to inspection'. He beats a hasty retreat as a plastic football narrowly misses his head and thuds into the wall.

At 7 p.m. prompt the Troop is paraded in a horseshoe formation and, miraculously, all is silent for the opening ceremony. The Union Jack is broken by the duty P.L. and saluted. The 'Parade Scouter' carries out a thorough personal inspection and the weekly bobs (shillings) are collected. Comments are made on the turnout, praise for the tidy, chastisement for the scruffy and those with missing items of uniform. Woggles seems to be the one thing that is most often missing.

During the fifteen minutes or so this is taking place, the 'Games Scouter' is busy outside preparing an event based on the Grand National which took place the previous Saturday. A course is marked out with water jumps (two ropes, three feet apart), fences (existing walls), ditches (forms), etc. When the Patrols arrive, their leaders are told to divide the boys into pairs for horses and riders. The race is run as a relay. Some horses fall at the first fence and those with jockeys as big as themselves find the going heavy. The race is finally won and, thankfully, no horses need to be put down. As the horses struggle for wind, I take advantage of the momentary lull to explain the next sequence of operations.

One Patrol is despatched indoors for a session of toffee making and another to the workshop for a talk on the use of saws, with an emphasis on safety, before being allowed to use a five foot, two-handed cross-cut saw on a railway sleeper. The best two boys are timed for this operation.

Meanwhile, on the road outside, a tin half filled with water and with a quantity of carbide attached to the underside of the lid is handed to another P.L. He and his patrol have to transport it on the trek cart round a circular course without activating the carbide and blowing off the lid! (There is a trek cart on the front cover of this book).

The other two Patrols are locked in combat over a game of skittle ball on the adjacent hard core car park. I arrive just in time to see three boys collide and limp to the side, clutching their injuries, with all the ballyhoo of professional footballers. They recover just as miraculously!

At thirty minute intervals Patrols change bases and at 8.45 p.m. all return to the H.Q. for results, comments etc.

Four trays of appetising, edible toffee are produced. Each Patrol having used the same recipe and ingredients, I wonder if the different colours concern hand hygiene, but Skip Bone assures me it's to do with the boiling! It all tastes good and is quickly devoured.

The Otter Patrol are successful with the bomb. Foxes are the slickest with the saw (55 seconds through the sleeper), Swifts the winners of the Grand National and Woodpigeons the master chefs.

It is 9 p.m. and the Troop is on parade again for the closing ceremony: announcements, flag down and prayers. Boys not dependent on transport are asked to help tidy up the H.Q. Back home for a well earned supper and a chance to reflect on the events of the evening! Soon it will be time to start thinking about next weeks programme.

Chapter Five

Our Own Place

As the Group grew, our thoughts turned to owning our own headquarters. The cash–strapped Y.M.C.A., now run by a part-time leader, was forced to hire out the meeting hall more and more and this had been a source of annoyance to me for some time. It all came to a head one winter's night, when I arrived early to set up for a meeting only to find that the hall had been double booked and was full of dogs! Cruft's Kendal was about to take place! All of our Leaders had experienced similar setbacks and we were tired of not having our own storage space on the premises and having to bring in everything needed for each meeting. The Group Council's concerns were shared by the Parents' Committee and so in 1958 we started seriously planning ways to make our dream come true.

Finding a suitable site proved difficult. We looked at several and were tempted by one close to the Drill Hall on Queen Katherine Street, but they all had serious drawbacks of one sort or another. It was 1960 before Kendal Town Council finally came to the rescue and offered us the Little Aynam site.

The old mill race, now the site of the Scout Hut.

Applications for planning permission were submitted to Westmorland County Council in June and again in October 1960 and were both refused. A third application was submitted on 9th December and permission for 'erection of a timber hut' finally granted in January 1961, but only for a five year period. The actual wording was: 'This approval shall expire on 31st December 1965 when the building shall be removed and the site cleared unless prior permission for its retention on the site for a further period is sought and obtained from the Local Planning Authority.' Two more conditions also applied: 'The building shall be maintained in a proper state of repair and decorative condition to the satisfaction of the Local Planning Authority' and 'The land shall be subject to a tree and shrub planting scheme etc...' The reasons for the conditions were (a) 'The building is to be constructed of materials which are liable to serious deterioration' and (b) 'To maintain control over the use of the site and to minimise injury to the visual amenities of the locality.' I believe that meant that it was not to spoil the view of the snuff works and other industrial buildings!

Now the real work began and every available hand was needed. The response to our call for help was excellent and soon Scouts, Leaders and parents were helping out evenings and weekends. The site, which had been part of a mill-race supplying power for a factory situated where Goodacre's now stands, had to be raised to the level of the road. We spent many weeks moving tons of rubble dumped by builders at our request. Using only picks and shovels and our bare hands, this was backbreaking work. In June 1961, I was quoted in The Lancashire Evening Post as saying that **only** another 30 tons of rubble was needed to complete the job and the site would be ready in two weeks! Thinking back I am amazed at what we achieved in this way. Incredible in this age of J.C.B.s!

It was a great day when G.F. Martindale and Sons, long-established Kendal builders, could finally make a start on the construction. In the late 1930s this firm had built Westmorland's impressive County Hall so we felt confident, almost honoured, to have them put up our humble 'timber hut'! Our architect, Michael Bunney, designed a building to provide a 50 ft. by 25 ft. hall, a small office, store, kitchen and toilets. Harry Anderson, grandfather of one of the Scouts and owner of Horncop Concrete Works, acted as our Clerk of Works and also donated all the boundary fencing. Thanks to Syd Turney's meticulous record keeping, we have the costings for all the work and they make interesting reading:

FINAL ESTIMATES FOR 1ST KENDAL GROUP HEADQUARTERS

M.J.H. Bunney, M.A., F.R.I.B.A.	Plans, Planning Permission	£10.17.6
G.F. Martindale and Sons Ltd.	Hut construction and erection Concrete raft, drains and rough casting	£1604.2.0
Jas. Williamson and Son Ltd, Lancaster	Covering to concrete floor (Done by Group)	£81.0.0
Builders Supply Co. (Kendal) Ltd.	Plumbing installation (Done by Group)	£77.7.6
North Western Electricity Board	Lighting and Heating installation	£145.10.0
North Western Electricity Board	Supplying Service to Headquarters	£ 21.12.6
Various	Garden Layout in Accordance with planning requirements. (Done by Group)	£ 50.0.0
Kendal Water Board	Water supply to Headquarters	£ 48.7.6
TOTAL		£2038.17.0

'Done by Group' denotes help given free of charge by parents and friends of the Group. All the plumbing work for example was done by Jim Clement, a partner in the well-known Kendal company W. Jackson and Co., who fitted into both these categories, being the treasurer of the Group for many years and also having a son in the Scouts. Williamsons of Lancaster, prominent vinyl floor makers at the time, supplied the flooring and allowed their employees to lay it in their spare time, subject to the Group providing transport and meals and payment of five shillings (25p) an hour! This was a very generous offer as the floor was quite a complicated piece of work, incorporating a mosaic depicting the Scout Fleur-de-Lis emblem. Being all hand-done, it was so labour intensive that the company had to turn down orders for other similar designs after a picture of it appeared in the national Scouting magazine. On the wall behind it Hiram Clement, brother of Jim, painted a mural showing Scouts from around the world enjoying a camp-fire.

Other donations included the Westmorland green slate from the Kirkstone quarries which was laid as crazy paving in front of the hut by John Newby, partner in the building firm Charnley, Purvis and Newby, whose son was

Exterior of Scout Hut on Little Aynam Road.
Courtesy Westmorland Gazette

Scout headquarters interior. Mural by Hiram Clement.
Courtesy Westmorland Gazette

also in the Scouts. A wooden flagpole, which had for years graced the tallest building in town, namely the Provincial Insurance Building, now found its way to our new headquarters. I say 'found its way', but we actually floated it down the river to its new home where it would be the crowning glory. Not, however, until another problem had been solved: how to build a strong enough support to hold erect a 25 ft. long 9 in. diameter flagpole, but again help arrived. Jack Dawson, a well-known farmers' blacksmith who had his premises at Longpool, not only designed and made the support, but came and erected it all free of charge. Fifty years on it is still doing its job, although the flagpole has been replaced. As the final touch, one of the Scouts by the name of Ian Ellison fashioned a wind vane for the roof of the building. It rested on ball-bearings from an old Sunderland aeroplane, which seems entirely appropriate since Ian went on to be commissioned in the Royal Air Force.

A grand opening of the new headquarters was finally held on the 20th October, 1962. The ceremony began with the breaking of the union flag on the flagpole outside the hut and the dedication of the headquarters by Canon Needham, Vicar of Kendal. The honour of actually opening the headquarters fell to a great benefactor of the Scouts. Mr. F. C. Scott, owner of the Provincial Insurance Company, had through the Frances Scott Trust Foundation provided us with an interest free loan without which the hut would not have become a reality at this time. One of the young Scouts handed the key to the headquarters to Mr. Scott who opened the door and went inside followed by special guests of the Group. These included the Mayor and Mayoress of Kendal, Mr. and Mrs. T. F. Sawyer, Mr. A. J. Anderson, chairman of the District Scout Association, Mr. L. Baron, County Commissioner of the Scout Movement and Mr. L. C. Reynolds, Headmaster of Kendal Grammar School and secretary to the County Association.

In their speeches the dignitaries praised the Scout Movement and the good work undertaken by Scouts. The Leaders of the 1st Kendal Troop and the Parents' Committee received praise for all their hard work and dedication. The following quotes are taken from an article in the Westmorland Gazette the following week:

'I was glad to be able to use some slight influence to grease some of the wheels which were being clogged and I hope the building will stand many years as a witness to those who pioneered it.' (The Mayor)

'I have been present at the opening of a number of Scout premises and I think this is the finest of them.' (Mr. L Baron)

'Kendal owes a debt of gratitude to the officers of this and other groups who have done so much for the right development of its youth.' (Mr. L Baron)

Tracing the development of Scouting in Kendal, Mr. W. Young, chairman of the 1st Kendal Group Committee, said he was surprised to find the first Kendal Scouts organisation was in existence as long ago as 1909, the first Kendal Scoutmaster, the late Mr. Gilbert Hogg, having been issued with his warrant on October 8th, 1909. The Kendal Scouts then used the 'tumble-down' Anchorite House, behind Kirkbarrow. In 1912 they went to Carlisle, where they were inspected by Baden-Powell, the Chief Scout. 'Lady Bagot consented to adopt the Troop,' Mr. Young went on, 'and she presented the first colours which had inscribed upon them 'Lady Bagot's Own'. After a little more history, Mr. Young thanked Mr. S. L. Turney for his untiring efforts in making the new headquarters a reality.

We now had a home for our 108 boys and their 13 Leaders, which was what the numbers had grown to in the span of nine years! It was very satisfying to be in this new building designed for our purposes, but within a few years it became necessary to build an addition to be used as a project room and store. In the Group publication 'Little Aynam News' (February 1968) Ken Hughes describes how this became a reality:

<u>HEADQUARTERS EXTENSION</u> (Project Room)

A cheerful cockney character breezed into the office. 'I've got a hut aboard me wagon, mate, where do you want it?' Oh happy Monday morning, our Project Room had arrived!

It didn't look very much like the substantial building we had in mind. 'Is it all there?' we enquired anxiously. 'It'll be all right, mate, when it's up,' assured our cheerful friend, and with the help of a second man he began to off-load at great speed. 'Will you be doing the erecting?' we asked. Not likely – we only deliver. The perishing erecting team should have been here to help us unload.' They unloaded and departed having obtained a signature for a heap of concrete slabs and bits and pieces.

At midday the two man erection team arrived and at once began to put the bits together. By evening it was beginning to look like a building. The weather was excellent throughout the week and by Friday their task was completed. The workmen were really sorry to leave and said they would have been quite happy to put up a building twice as large in such pleasant surroundings.

The windows were to be glazed by ourselves as this item was not included in the contract job. A phone call to Mr. Clement and W. Jackson & Co. had the job done almost before the phone was replaced. Such excellent service is much appreciated.

At the weekend Skip (Steptoe) Cannon called upon his many contacts and produced a variety of useful cupboards, fixtures and fittings. These were soon installed in the Project Room together with more items which had been stored in the main building. We cannot remember when the main hall last looked so tidy and uncluttered.

As some of the Scouts were on half-term holiday they were organised into a painting gang to deal with the first coat on all the woodwork (both inside and outside). We must particularly mention their names because they did a very good job, confining the paint to those places where it was intended to be (not always an easy task for Scouts). Well done, Brian Wilson, Alistair Bain, Malcolm Fraser, Tony Heslop and Harry Howson!

We still have to see to the electrical installation but already this is being actively undertaken by Skip Bone and his 'Electrical' Sub-committee.

Although there is a lot to be done before the job is finally completed we can with considerable satisfaction report that the 'Project Room' is now operational.

When I tell you that one of my ongoing projects was building canoes, you will understand Ken's excitement finally to have my 'projects' out of the main hall!

Although the project room is occasionally still used on meeting nights, its main use is for storing canoes and large camping equipment and as a garage for the Group's minibus.

Sixty years on the building is still in good condition. The original lino floor is still there, but covered by parquet wood flooring, and Hiram Clement's mural has been painted over and replaced by the Scout emblem.

Surely this is worth more than a bob! John Francis does his bit for Bob-a-Job Week.

Courtesy Westmorland Gazette

Chapter Six

Bob-a-Job and other Money Making Activities

At the end of the war the Scout Movement was in the same economic state as the country. It was conscious of the need to develop its activities and it looked for new sources of income. When someone suggested sending out all Scouts and Cubs in the land to do jobs for people in return for only one shilling (5p) per job, there must have been a lot of scepticism. I doubt if many could have foreseen how successful this idea would prove. Bob-a-Job Week was launched! It was always held in Easter week and continued from 1949 till the early seventies, although by then it had been renamed 'Scout Job Week'. A set portion of the money earned went directly to National Headquarters. I am not sure what this was in 1949, but in 1970 it was 10 shillings (50p) per boy. When you consider that the total membership then was almost certainly in excess of 400,000, you will see that the revenue generated by this simple effort was considerable – approximately £200,000, a considerable amount in today's terms, but of course an even more impressive amount back then.

In the 'Little Aynam News', Spring 1970 edition, David Bone wrote a thank you to the people who had helped during Scout Job Week, not only those directly connected with the Group, but also the general public who made an effort to find jobs for the boys to do. Looking through the job cards, which had to be signed by the recipient of the service, he found that the main occupations had been 'car washing and sweeping of paths to babysitting and measuring of land.' He goes on to say, 'It would appear that the old Bob-a-Job theme is still our public image since most individual donations were ONE SHILLING. Nevertheless, the average per boy amounted to £1. 9s. 0d. (£1.45) of which 10s. (50p) is payable to Headquarters, London, leaving an average earning for the Troop of 19s. (95p) per boy.'

He also had an idea about changing the time of this annual event and suggested that a fortnight rather than just a week would be better as long as it was in the summer, when 'people are more tolerant and can think of 1001 jobs that ought to be done.' 'Just as it isn't right,' he goes on, 'to ask people to leave the warmth of the fireplaces to look out some work for the Scouts, nor is it reasonable to send boys on frustrating job-hunting expeditions in extreme weather conditions - hail, rain, snow and blow!'

One job David didn't mention was dog-walking, but when a lady on Sunnyside struggled to find an instant job for nine-year-old Geoffrey, that was the one that sprang to mind. She handed over her beloved pooch and asked him to take it for a walk on nearby Castle Hill. He left with clear instructions ringing in his ears not to let the dog off the lead. All went well until, nearing the castle ruins, a stray dog came into sight and Geoffrey's charge broke free and took off on the run, complete with lead. It was a somewhat subdued young boy who went back to Sunnyside to explain what had happened, but such was the regard for the Scouts, that the kind lady still signed his card and gave him two shillings!

The older the boys got, the more reluctant they were to knock on doors asking for jobs, so for my Senior Scouts I used to line up bigger jobs requiring our combined efforts. This way we had some good learning experiences while earning more than our share of the capitation amount due. The picture below shows one of these instances – where twelve Senior Scouts and I spent the weekend felling and logging a tall tree for Fred Simpson, Brigsteer Road, Principal of Kendal College.

Brian Elshaw and David Cutt hard at work.

It is generally said that Bob-a-Job Week died out with decimalization, but I think it had as much to do with concerns for the safety of the boys. Fifty years ago parents encouraged their children to play outside with their pals and we had no worries about our lads seeking work from virtual strangers.

With what we know today about 'stranger danger', of course we could no longer contemplate this.

The need to raise funds is, of course, a necessary evil for most organisations and we were no different. It wasn't all bad though, as a lot of fun was had in amongst the hard work. Today it seems that with the faster pace of life, more mothers out at work and so on, parents will rather pay higher subs and not have to become involved in such activities, but I do think they are missing out on a lot. Through working together toward a common goal many friendships were formed amongst the parents and between Leaders and parents.

Anybody who was involved in the fifties, sixties and seventies will never forget the many jumble sales where a rag and bone man and local character would promise to 'come and pick up our remains' at the end of the day. One mother who deserves a special mention is Mrs. Doris Sharpe who for several years organised the auctioning of the better items, always obtaining the optimum price.

When sponsored walks and swims became popular, we did those too! In 1968 we even held a sponsored crisp eating competition, the idea coming from Eric Laycock, manager of the Kendal branch of the Bradford and Bingley Building Society. According to Ken Hughes' report in the 'Little Aynam News', the Scouts who ate the most bags of crisps in the allotted time of 15 minutes were Maurice Williams and Philip Sharpe at eight bags each. Apparently Ken and I managed six bags each, but didn't have much sponsorship! The most money was raised by a Cub Scout, Paul Sedgwick, who was sponsored at over 30 bob a bag (£1.50)!

We held pony gymkhanas, dances and barbecues! We planted trees at Limefitt Caravan Park, and who can forget the collection of Green Shield Stamps? Our annual Christmas coffee morning in the Town Hall was always well attended, and Kath Bainbridge and Janet Hughes have over the years raised huge amounts by organising the sale of Christmas cards and gifts. Although some of these activities are still happening, fewer parents are involved today. I believe this is a pity, also for the sake of the boys, as doing something along with their parents – even working together at a coffee morning – is something children love.

The Whole Gang 1959

Chapter Seven

Gang Shows

I am intrigued by the way some events that start out small and unsuccessful manage to grow and become quite important. In 1954 Margaret Hall thought it would be good if around a dozen Cubs and Scouts could provide an evening's entertainment for parents by way of thanking them for their fund raising efforts and support. 'Just a few small sketches and some campfire songs,' she said, adding, 'Oh, and I've got someone who will help with the singing.' Margaret's powers of persuasion are well-known. The 'someone' turned out to be Stan Walling, a manager at the Provincial Insurance Company and the organist of the Presbyterian Church on Sandes Avenue. In his younger days he had been actively involved in local amateur dramatics. Margaret had struck gold again! The following month we rehearsed the sketches in different parents' homes and some costumes were made. Stan somehow managed to train a good little choir in spite of having to use the Y.M.C.A.'s out of tune piano.

Zion Sunday School room in the New Inn Yard was booked, but, unfortunately, on the day of the show, following prolonged rainfall, the River Kent burst its banks! Miller Bridge and Stramongate Bridge became unusable, resulting in people living on the east side of town being prevented from crossing to the west where the entertainment was to take place. It badly affected our audience and also deprived us of some key performers. However, undaunted and in the true tradition of the theatre, the show went on! It could hardly be described as a success, but parents made allowances and were generous with their applause. You would have thought that the chaotic events of that evening would have put paid to any further theatrical ideas, but instead it, unbelievably, heralded the start of a series of Gang Shows that would continue until 1963.

The shows always took place in December and the early ones were presented in the Oddfellows Hall on Highgate Bank, which was rented by the Y.M.C.A. With a cast of fifty boys in 1956, it grew to seventy in 1960 and topped one hundred in 1962. As the numbers increased, we were forced to look for larger venues. Shows were staged at the Parish Hall, the Town Hall, and for the last three years we hired the 399 seat main hall at Longlands Girls School (now part of Queen Katherine School) on two nights - quite a change from that early flood affected evening back in 1954! The cost of hiring the Longlands Hall was £15.5s!

Mike Sagar, Mike Molloy, John Barber and Mike Allen, with Vivian Eddleston at the piano, singing 'Love, Love, Love.

'Mama don't allow no jazz band playing in here' performed by Bruce Cowperthwaite on banjo, Bill Duff on clarinet, Mike Molloy on trumpet, Mike Sagar on piano, Mike Allen on washboard, Bill Gilpin on trombone, and Alan Baker on string bass.

Stan Walling, our producer and pianist, was the mainstay of each Gang Show and his work was beyond praise. All three sections of the Group: Cubs, Scouts and Senior Scouts contributed items and many rehearsals took place in parents' homes. For the grand opening every boy and Leader was on stage and it called for a skilled organiser to get us seated. Syd Turney with his vast military training was the obvious choice. At the 1959 show in the Parish Hall, Syd expertly tiered us up in five rows. As he made the final adjustments, he stepped back into the closed curtains and disappeared from view to land in front of the surprised audience. He reappeared shortly, shaken but, thankfully, unhurt; saved no doubt by his wartime parachute training.

My own childhood interest in things theatrical was nil. I was once cast as a rabbit at St. George's C. of E. Primary School and I recall refusing to wear the costume that the part required. Miss Elson, Headteacher, was summonsed to resolve this little difficulty. She was a formidable lady and we were all scared of her. However, on this occasion, I stood my ground and landed one of my little pals with the part – and the costume! By the time the Gang Shows came along, I had overcome my childhood stage phobia and happily duetted with Mike Sagar and did whatever Stan Walling directed. The programme for our 1959 show gives some idea of the sort of entertainment we provided and the work involved in staging the performance:

INTRODUCTION

Take one genius called Ralph Reader, who started Gang Shows back in the 1930s, and squeeze out about two hours of stock with meat, sweeten and season to taste. Collect seventy collected Cubs, Scouts and Senior Scouts with kindly parents and leave to soak in the stock for two and a half months. Secure Stan Walling as chef, Margaret Hall, Ken Hughes and Jim Cannon as under-chefs and allow them at regular and frequent intervals to grind Cubs and Scouts, remove raw edges and stir in more stock till all dissolves. Mix well with tender music from Vivian Eddleston (a sixth form girl from Kendal High School) in favourable atmosphere of rehearsal venues as it is essential at this stage to keep cool. When stock begins to bubble, increase the heat steadily, the fire being stoked by stalwarts Clarry Walker, Terry Howarth and David Bone, garnish with pieces of furniture and props from a variety of well-wishers. Peel the boys and coat with fancy covers and icing from Barbara Hughes and fifty mums. Pour the mixture into the Parish Bowl and, with the help of Syd Turney and company, staff the front of house and back stage. Bring to the boil and stir violently, until mixture pours smoothly. Serve with menu a la Dorothy Dixon. The whole makes a delicious and appetising confection if served piping hot.

At this point I must take the opportunity to acknowledge all the help given to me by my friend Dorothy Dixon. We worked together in the Education Department at the County Hall, and for years she spent her lunch hours and any spare minute typing camp programmes and menus, our monthly newsletter, Gang Show programmes and song sheets etc. When my wife was typing the following programme from the 1960 Gang Show, she wished she had Dorothy's speed and expertise.

PROGRAMME

1.	Opening Chorus:		The Company
	Looking High, High, High		
2.	Twelve Days of Camping		I. Ellison, A. Cannan, A. Somes,
			J. Campbell, J. Reed, T. Harris, L. Porter,
			K. Williams, T. Hughes, A. Barber, D. Tebay
3.	Dobbin Does It Again		A. Yates, I. Rigg, P. Rigg, D. Biddulph,
			I. Armstrong, G. Gordon, P. Briggs,
			J. Williams, A. Aplin
4.	We're a Couple of Swells		M. Sagar, E. Greenwood
5.	Ideal Camps	S. Master	J. Cannon
		P. Leader	I. Ellison
		Scouts	J. Reed, L. Porter, K. Williams,
			J. Campbell, A. Barker
6.	Michael Finnigan		E. Greenwood, A. Powell, I. Rigg,
	Land of the Silver Birch		P. Reynolds, S. Sproat, M. Black,
			C. Hayton, A. Cannan
7.	Meet the Navy		The Company

INTERMISSION

8.	Gypsy Rovers:	J. Barber, M. Allen, M. Powell, T. Cotton,
	(The Whistling Gypsy,	J. Reed, D. Orrick, L. Porter, T. Hughes,
	Apache,	D. Tebay, K. Williams, M. Powell,
	With the Scent of Woodsmoke)	J. Campbell, A. Somes
9.	Atmospherics	J. Duff, D. Dunbar, I. Durston, D. Cutt
10.	Bob-a-Job	J. Cannon, M. Sagar, J. Barber and members
		of A Troop.
		Trio: J. Campbell, M. Powell, D. Tebay
11.	Black and White	Terry (Jolson) Howarth
12.	Count Your Chicks	E. Greenwood, A. Powell, P. Reynolds,
		I. Rigg, S. Sproat, M. Black, C. Hayton,
		A. Cannan
13.	Golden Days	B Troop
14.	Hippopotamus Song	J. Barber, M. Sagar, J. Cannon
	Goodness Gracious Me	J. Cannon, M. Sagar
	Standing on the Corner	M. Allen, J. Barber, M. Molloy, M. Sagar
15.	Favourites from Fifty Nine	The Company

THE QUEEN

I see from the minutes of a Group Leaders meeting that in January 1961 we presented excerpts from the show at Maude's Meadow Hospital; Kendal Green Hospital; Ethel Hedley Children's Orthopaedic Hospital, at Calgarth near Windermere; Abbey Home at Staveley and Kendal Over Sixties Club.

I still remember the words to many of the songs and sketches we did over the years, but will spare my readers from including them here. There is one poem, however, which stands out in my mind. It was read by Antony Jay on B.B.C. 'Tonight' on Tuesday 26th September 1961 and was recited by Eldred Himsworth at the last Gang Show we did. It deals with the change from short trousers to long, but another three years would pass before longs became part of the official Scout uniform.

Behold them – they will soon be gone –
The shorts we built our Empire on!
What further proof need be displayed
That Britain's greatness has decayed
Now that we see, on leg of Scout,
That slack is in and short is out.

It's time that Britons turned their thoughts
To the advantages of shorts.
As every boy finds out at school
They're economical and cool,
No turn-ups to get in the way
Or fill with fluff, or fall, or fray.
And pious folk are well aware,
Their creases are not lost in prayer.

But do not think we've only lost
Coolness, convenience and cost.
As Shorts at last recede from view,
The spirit has departed too;
These were the shorts that sailed the seas
With gallant empire – building knees
That strode through jungle, sand and plain
With mule and horse and camel-train;
They filled the world, these British shorts,
With cricket fields and tennis courts.

JIM WANTS TO KNOW:
If this would be considered
a bad camp sight?

A world of sahibs and chota pegs
And knobbly knees and hairy legs
Which in white duck and khaki drill
Enforced the great Imperial will.
And as they take their final bow
We ask, 'Where is the Empire now?'

The naked knee, the stockinged calf –
Today they only raise a laugh;
The slack and, even more obscene,
The transatlantic canvas jean,
They clothe the nation's legs today
And shorts have all but passed away.

And yet the torch is not quite out;
On schoolboy and on junior Scout
The badge of empire still holds sway,
The famous flag still flies today.
So here's our final clarion call –
Britannia's shorts must never fall!

In 1964, after a run of eight years, the shows came to an end. They had served us well. We had raised the profile of the Group and gained many new friends and supporters as well as having raised a significant amount of money towards the cost of our new headquarters.

Chapter Eight

Tarn Hows – A little piece of Heaven!

Generations of former Kendal Guides will remember Miss Dinsdale with affection. Her whole life was inextricably linked with Guiding, a Brownie in 1921, a Guide in 1924 and a Ranger in 1931. When she was granted her first Leader's warrant with the 1st Kendal Y.W.C.A. Company in 1932 at the age of twenty, it was the start of a Guiding journey that would last for 55 years. My earliest memories of this petite lady go back to the war years, when she was Captain of the 1st Natland Guides and I was a boy in the Scouts. Each Christmas a party for both Guides and Scouts would be held in the village school. There would be games with prizes and somehow our mothers always managed to conjure up a wonderful tea in spite of war rationing.

In the summer we would join together for a game of netball and I still remember being rebuked by Miss Dinsdale for knocking the ball out of the girls' hands and using body contact!

Throughout the war and up to the early fifties, Kendal Guides made good use of a small cabin located at the north end of Tarn Hows. It was made available by the generosity of the Scott family at Matson Ground. Marjorie Walker, wife of Clarry, who was a Ranger in the 8th Kendal, recalls many happy weekends spent there. On bank holidays the girls would cycle there on the Friday night carrying well-packed rucksacks. On hot days they would swim in the tarn, but only when Miss Dinsdale was present as she possessed the necessary life saving certificate. Sunday mornings would see them walk to church at Hawkshead and in the afternoon they would often cycle to Grasmere. Monday they would have to cycle all the way back again. I don't think Guides today would be up to that or, indeed, would be allowed to do it because of safety concerns. It was actually those concerns that made Marjorie Dinsdale give up using the site and offer it to us. As it had been for the Guides, it became a very popular destination for us Scouts also, but I must admit that we never went there on our bikes!

Although I personally have a lot of very happy memories from Tarn Hows, I could not express them as well as one of my Scouts from those days, Alan Baker, whose contributions to the writing of this book have been most appreciated. Over to Alan:

TARN HOWS – AN EARTHLY PARADISE

Little known to the hordes who do the circuit of Tarn Hows on the public path is

*Marjorie Dinsdale (on the left) with the Westmorland County Standard
at the Dedication Service 1953.*

Courtesy of Beryl Dinsdale

The hut at Tarn Hows.

the hidden gem of a smaller tarn in a hollow near the north end, together with a fenced off private compound and a little wooden hut. For many years, the 1st Kendal Scouts made excellent use of this facility, spending days, weekends and weeks there, to the extent that for some of us it became almost home from home. We certainly got to know the surrounding terrain like the backs of our proverbial hands.

The hut was somewhat primitive in its facilities, but was ideal for a group of adventure seeking boys. It had a small communal room with a fireplace that gushed smoke profusely, over which many a dixieful of strong stew was brewed. There were two small bunkrooms and a tiny storeroom. At the far end of the compound was the usual primitive arrangement of a small wooden closet, lacking only the traditional crescent moon cut-out in the door. At least it was more than is provided in the 21st century for the thousands of tourists who visit Tarn Hows every year.

The tarn was a magical place, especially at early dawn, when mists would swoop off the surrounding fells and bank up over the water in spooky formations; or in the depths of winter, when no-one was about and all that could be heard was the creaking of ice – and the shouting of Scouts playing a primitive form of ice hockey.

The location was absolutely ideal for learning all the basic skills of outdoor life, camping and cooking, camp hygiene (yes, even us lads could be taught the value of cleanliness), knots and lashings, stalking, building tree houses, rafting and canoeing. And of course, with all the surrounding fells, there was lots of scope for fell walking and hiking.

Some things were learnt the hard way. On one occasion, we had three patrol tents spaced out around the small tarn, having selected our sites on a lovely sunny afternoon. Unfortunately, the sunny afternoon translated into a wild and stormy night, and when the occupants of one tent were blithely informed by Stan Hooton, the Troop sage, 'I don't want to worry you lads, but that creaking noise is the two trees above you, which are just managing to stop each other from falling over' – that was the signal to a) panic, b) decamp, and c) resolve never to camp under trees again.

In the earliest days, before every household had a car or two, transport was a problem, but thanks to the generosity of the Westmorland Gazette, we often used their old yellow van to get all our gear there. Getting ourselves there could be another problem. I remember walking there from Kendal with Bill Duff and camping overnight at Great Tower en route. (Why is it part of the natural law that

A game of quoits when Marjorie Dinsdale and Guides visited the Scouts at Tarn Hows.

On the ferry going to Tarn Hows: Ian Ellison, Howard Whitehurst, Jim Duff (Dr. Jim on the recent BBC 2 show 'Extreme Dreams with Ben Fogle'), Alan Park, Geoff Dunbar and Roger Dangerfield.

your first day out, and only the first day, will see you soaked to the skin, so that you spend the rest of the time trying to dry out?)

The only transport anyone possessed was Jim's D.M.W. motorbike, which was not exactly ideal when emergencies cropped up. One day, Jim and all the lads except Alan Troughton and me, who were on cooking duty, had set off to the far end of the tarn to launch a raft, when they were disturbed by our urgent shouts of 'Skip, Skip'. On rushing back to the hut, they found that Clarry, our assistant S.M., had almost severed his thumb with a felling axe, which he had been using to cut firewood. With his thumb swathed in bandages and tea towels, he was last seen on the pillion seat of Jim's bike, holding his thumb aloft like a bloody trophy and bouncing into the distance on the way to Kendal Hospital. Of course, this was in the days before Health and Safety experts had been invented! (Clarry spent a week in hospital but, thankfully, his thumb was saved).

The daily routine at Tarn Hows was, as at all our camps, strictly (?) observed, with rotas, routines, times for formalities, times for fun. Every day, two of us had the chore of walking to Hawkshead Hill Farm and back for fresh milk, and every Sunday, we would all walk to Hawkshead in our best uniforms to go to church. An opportunity to spend what money we had in the shops at the same time!

One memorable event took place at Tarn Hows, which has stayed in the memory of the few who took part in a strange night out. A group of us left Kendal on the late night bus for Ambleside with the intention of walking through the countryside at night and ending up in the wee small hours at the hut. Such night hikes were often undertaken quite safely in those days. However, on leaving Ambleside, the snow started to fall quite briskly and we eventually found ourselves at Skelwith Bridge, having narrowly avoided walking into the lake at Rydal. From there we walked along the road to High Arnside, and then followed the lane that passes near the north end of Tarn Hows. By this time, the snow was about 6 inches deep, when a most bizarre event occurred. In the pitch black of a dark winter's night, the whole sky, the whole landscape, suddenly lit up as bright as day for about 5-10 seconds. There was no apparent source of light – quite simply, the whole world was just illuminated, and we could see to the furthest horizons. We all just stood stock still in the light and the silence, hardly daring to breathe. And years later, it is only when any two of us have met, we have to ask ourselves, 'Did that really happen?' And the answer is 'Yes, it did,' but none of us can offer any explanation for it. It was seen by those who were walking, and by Jim and Clarry who were waiting for us at the hut. Spooky!

Our stays at Tarn Hows gave us ample opportunity to indulge in that great favourite of Scouting activities – wide games. The terrain around the tarn is absolutely ideal for those adventurous games where we had to pit our wits against the wiles of our enemies, making the best possible use of rock and hollow, stream and tree. What better excuse for letting off lots of steam and getting really dirty? And what better way to learn how to love and make good use of the countryside, and to use one's initiative?

Senior Scout John Barber with Jim Duff, Barry Link and Anthony Clement practicing back woods camping.

Tarn Hows must rank with Ashness Bridge as one of the most photographed scenes in the Lake District. It is probably also one of the most visited beauty spots – a place where thousands of people exchange their money for the privilege of parking and strolling along the well-made paths, which are even accessible to wheelchairs. It is a delightful place, and it is good that people are made so welcome there and are able to enjoy what we as young lads were privileged to have almost to ourselves 50 years ago.

Chapter Nine

Variety is the Spice of Life!

Boys join the Scouts for a variety of reasons, but nearly all expect adventure, excitement, fun and friendship. To fulfil these aspirations the poor old Scout Leader needs constantly to think of new things to do and it is vital that he supplements his ideas with help from outside sources. It is a never-ending job, but it pays good dividends. Some of the more memorable activities were run by parent volunteers over an ongoing period of time, while others came about almost by chance and were usually done in a day.

On one occasion, for example, my ears pricked up when I heard a leader from the Young Farmers' Club mention a hill farmer somewhere 'up North' who did pony trekking at a very reasonable cost. I wasted no time in giving him a call. Yes, he could take up to a maximum of sixteen at a time. It was probably best if they were thirteen years or older, and they didn't need any former experience. He charged 10/6d. (53p) for about a three hour trek. Too good to be true! I mentioned this at the next Troop meeting and I had a full posse of deputies straight away, subject to consent from Mum and Dad, of course. When I later contacted the farmer to confirm the booking, he said, 'Mind on thoo weers lang britches, er yer legs'll git aw chapped.'

One sunny Saturday morning around Easter time, armed with a packed lunch and carrots for the horses (Scout law number six: A Scout is a friend to animals), we climbed aboard our trusty ambulance and headed out of town anticipating a grand adventure. The destination was a hill farm a few miles from Appleby and we were told to turn down a farm track when we got to a Dutch barn. The twenty-five mile journey to Appleby winds its way through some spectacular countryside before joining Boroughgate, described by Alfred Wainwright as Westmorland's finest street. From the gates of Appleby Castle it sweeps down majestically to the historic church of Saint Lawrence by the River Eden. As a lead-in for high adventure on horseback this journey takes some beating. Shortly after leaving Appleby sixteen pairs of eyes had no difficulty at all in spotting our landmark. The Dutch barn leant over at an alarming angle and looked ready to fall down at any moment. It had ropes fastened to the pillars supporting the roof and it was clear that some time ago an attempt had been made to stop further movement. The farmer had now clearly resigned himself to the inevitable, as the ropes hung down limply. We Scouts know a great deal about guy

Bruce Cowperthwaite being hoisted from a raft on to the footbridge near Sedgwick.

lines as they are the things that hold up our tents, but there was no time for good deeds today!

As we arrived at the gate to the farmyard, we saw an amazing collection of horses: big ones, small ones, fat ones, skinny ones, piebald, skewbald, rough coated, smooth coated and even a little palomino. Over by the far gate stood an almost black horse, taller than the others, handsome and aloof! Surveying the scene I had a feeling of having been transported back in time. There were no signs of modern day equipment to be seen, not even an old Land Rover. This feeling did not change when the farmer emerged from his house. He was wearing an army greatcoat, tied around the middle with a bit of binder twine. He invited us Leaders in for a cup of coffee while the boys were left to acquaint themselves with their transport. We followed our host into the main room of the house where all the daily living took place. It took a little time before we could see what the room was like as it was very dark, owing to the thickness of the walls and the windows being very small. Most of one wall was taken up by a huge, raised fireplace on which burned the largest log I had ever seen. When I remarked on this, the farmer replied, 'Aye, yon fire hessn't bin oot fer three 'eer.' Alongside the smouldering log was a very black coffee pot, similar to the ones you see in cowboy films. I had often wondered what that must have tasted like, and I was soon to find out. It was foul! It put a lining in my mouth and coated everything it touched on the way down. Perhaps that is why I now only drink tea?

Back outside, slapping one of the horses hard on its rump sending up a huge cloud of dust, the farmer said, 'Seesta, Ah've given them aw a gud dustin, sea thoo waint catch owt smittle.' I suppose he had used a powder to kill off any lice or similar pests, but the dust did nothing for my asthma! While we were in the house, the boys had been getting to know the horses and had already picked their favourites. The horses also seemed quite attached to the boys, but that may have had something to do with the treats the boys had been giving them. These were meant for the lunch break out on the trail! All the pairing up had been for nothing, however, as the farmer asked, 'Whea's bin ev a nag afoor?' He naturally wanted the experienced boys to go on the more spirited horses. The most coveted steed was the palomino with the kind of saddle used by cowboys already on its back. This saddle distinguished itself from the others by having a pair of chaps (not leather, but felt) attached to it as well as a pommel just waiting for a lasso. John Capstick was the lucky lad chosen and was the envy of all the rest. The farmer's method of pairing up man and beast was, however, far from foolproof. In spite of the fact that I told him my only experience of riding had been on the donkeys on the sands at Morecambe many years - or should I say donkey's years? - ago, I still got landed with Prince, the handsome big stallion mentioned above!

Pony trekking near Appleby. Prince and I had cleared the water hazard and were way out in front.

With a leg-up from my new friend, the farmer, I soon found myself astride Prince. The view from his back was great, but I was also very aware that the ground was a long way below me. At this point I was rather too preoccupied with my own situation to pay much attention to the boys, but they all seemed to have managed to mount their horses with much less difficulty. The moment the farm gate was opened, Prince relived his glory-days on the racetrack and took off at a tremendous rate. I clung on doggedly, looking in vain for the brake, and found myself coming down as the horse was coming up. The meeting every time that happened caused considerable pain! Soon we got to a small stream, but that didn't slow him down. Oh, no, he went through it full gallop, water flying everywhere. Eventually the farmer caught up with Prince and me and brought us to a halt. He proceeded to tell me off, 'Divvent thee mek him gallop, er thoo'll set aw t'lot off!' – as if I had anything to do with it! He was mistaken anyway, because, looking back, I saw a long way behind the rest of the horses plodding along slowly, showing no inclination to break into a gallop. Having shown what he could do, Prince was now happy to go along at a more sedate pace. The next mile or so was quite flat and I was warming to the whole idea when we took a sharp right and headed for the hills. Our progress got slower and slower and soon the farmer announced that we would have to dismount and lead our horses on foot. After a while, we reached the snowline and the farmer suggested we stop to eat our sandwiches. Having found a sheltered place, I dusted off a big stone and sat myself down. It was good to find something to sit on that didn't move. The pleasure was to be short-lived, though, as the farmer spotted me and called out, 'Divvent thee ga sitten' ev that cau'd steane, mi lad, er thoo'll end up wid piles!' His concern for my welfare was touching, but at that time the possibility of getting haemorrhoids was the least of my worries! Having told the boys to make sure to bring treats for their horses, I now, embarrassingly, found that I had forgotten to do so myself. In desperation I broke off a piece of my emergency ration of Kendal Mint Cake for Prince to try. He munched on it slowly, coughed and spat it out! Then he turned his head to fix me with his big, dark eye, as if to say, 'Now let's have a Mars Bar to get rid of that awful taste.' He settled for one of my beef sandwiches and I bit into the mint cake.

Feeling refreshed, or at least less hungry, we proceeded to the summit, still leading our horses. The wonderful views from up here offered some compensation for our discomfort. We carried on a little way down the other side before remounting. From here on, we were able to stay on the horses all the way back to the farm. By now some of the riders were more comfortable and able to go a little faster and by the time these brave souls reached the farm, our little group was strung out for what seemed like miles. We looked like Napoleon's retreat from Moscow! Long after the stragglers had arrived back, Clifford Williams, a Young Leader, hove into view, leading his horse, which had run out of steam and refused to carry him for the last few miles. The boys all agreed that it had indeed been a grand adventure and some were ready to go again, but I am afraid it would have had to be without this Leader! 'Comfortable' is not a word I would use about the way I was feeling, but that was to be as nothing compared to the way I felt for days after my experience! When eventually I was able to sit astride my motorcycle, it felt good, knowing that I had full control over its movements and in particular the brakes. Need I say that I have kept well away from horses ever since?

Another of these one-off, special events came about through my contact with Tony Booth, the School Enquiry Officer for North Westmorland. Tony, who was also a Territorial Army Officer, arranged for us a visit to Warcop Gunnery Range to watch tanks firing armour-piercing shells. Twenty-two boys assembled at our H.Q. on Saturday, 12th March, 1966 and left in the

Terry Howarth under snow ball attack at Great Tower.

Winter fun above Shap; Julian Dwane, Gordon Dwane, Paul Howe, Stephen Hunter, Craig Hunter, Mark Nicholson and Harry Hanson.

ambulance and Skip Hughes' car. At Warcop we were met by Tony who gave us an interesting talk on the various features of the 46-ton tanks. We then stuffed cotton wool in our ears before the guns, which have a range of 7,000 yards (Staveley to Kendal), roared into action. From our vantage point overlooking the four tanks we were able to see the red-hot shells rocketing through the air and thudding with deadly accuracy into the targets which were old tanks strewn over the limestone fellside. Altogether 1,200 shells were fired and at a cost of around £38 each, more than most would earn in a week, – well, a lot of money was blasted off! When the firing was over, the Scouts were shown around the tanks. The whole scene would have given Giles plenty of material for a good cartoon!

Back at the camp, a hot stew was ready for us at the cookhouse. Ken and I were introduced to two members of the staff, a Major and a Regimental Sergeant Major, who had both been Scouts. The R.S.M. was able to reel off the ten Scout Laws after a lapse of over thirty years, a feat so remarkable that I still remember it after another forty!

After conveying our thanks, we left for Kirkby Stephen to see the Potter brothers' fine collection of vintage motorbikes, cars and fire engines. It had been a day full of excitement and interest for Scouts and Leaders alike.

Throughout the history of the 1st Kendal, fell walking has been a major activity, and in a report written by Syd Turney in 1964 it says: 'We are fortunate in having the services of two lay helpers, Mr. A. Day and Mr. J. Wilson from the Provincial Insurance Company, who have been taking the oldest boys on the Lakeland Fells and giving them a sound grounding in map reading and compass work and, perhaps most of all, a sound knowledge of the code of safety for fell walkers.' In the early seventies their good work was continued by John Atkinson, the genial owner of Kendal Sport Shop, with help from parents of some of the Scouts, most notably David Watson, Danny Thompson, Glyn Harris and Norman Sharpe. They kicked off with a walk to Helm Crag, affectionately known as the Lion and the Lamb. In the following weeks they tackled a variety of routes, including following the River Kent from its source down through Staveley and Burneside to Kendal. Some weekend camps were held and from one at Wasdale climbs were made to Great Gable, Scafell Pike and Haystacks. After a hike to the Stone Axe Factory on the screes of Pike o' Stickle, John noticed that one boy kept falling behind. He decided to help the boy by carrying his rucksack for a while and he soon discovered the reason for the lad's lack of progress. The rucksack was half full of prehistoric stone axes! After jettisoning all but two of his best finds, all was well.

Rodney Woodhouse spinning a lasso.

A good turn. Peter Briggs and Tim Molloy using a cross cut saw to log up a fallen tree at Tarn Hows.

John's walking companion was Sarah, his Jack Russell dog. On one hike, which involved crossing a scree, her paws became very sore and she had difficulty walking. Clifford Williams came to the rescue when he resolutely placed Sarah in his rucksack, the draw cord tied around her neck, and carried her all the way back to the Land Rover.

Between 1977 and 1980 fellwalking became the responsibility of Bill Brown, an engineer with North Western Water Authority, who held the Mountain Leadership Certificate. He was helped by a group of fellwalking dads: Tony Barber, Jim Plenderleith, John Hamer, Richard Horsley, Ron Starkey, George Ellwood and Brian Booth. Hikes took place from late September through to spring to a variety of destinations such as Coniston Old Man, Ingleborough, Wet Sleddale, Kentmere and Helvellyn. On the hikes they would occasionally encounter snow and, being Scouts, they would be prepared and be carrying sleds in their pockets. A plastic bag has an endless number of uses!

Using K Fellfarers' Hostel at Seathwaite as a base, many boys had the opportunity to climb to the summits of Scafell and Great Gable. Having conquered England's highest peak, the mountains of Scotland beckoned. They camped at Glen Nevis and climbed to the summit of Ben Nevis. On the way down they came upon a lady who had broken her ankle. As this was before the advent of mobile phones, two of the lads, Jonathan Lacey and David Lecore, were despatched down the mountain to call out the rescue team, while the rest of the boys made her comfortable. What luck! To be able to put into practice what you had learned in theory! 1st Kendal received a commendation from the Fort William Police for their swift action.

Although the following activity was run by the Leaders and not by volunteers, I still want to include it in this chapter, as it very much involved the fathers of the Scouts; it was, in fact, a Father and Son Camp, the only one I remember us ever running. It wasn't just any ordinary camp either, but a Challenge Camp, and, looking back, I see that we certainly set the fathers some quite challenging tasks. They will have come away from the weekend with a good knowledge of what their boys got up to when they left them in our 'tender' care for a week at a time! The following report gives a father's perspective as it was written by one of the participants, Glyn Harris, County Schools Advisor, and father of Chris.

DAD'S ARMY

Recently I have returned to the peace and tranquillity of Westmorland after twenty years spent in the noise and bustle of London. That peace and tranquillity was

The Summit of Helvellyn. We were made of tough stuff in those days. L/R Alan Baker, Bill Duff, John Barber, Geoff Waterworth, Mike Molloy, Bill Gilpin and Jim.

Walking the high fells: Graham Starkey, David Kelly, Jonathan Lacey and Mark Nicholson.
Courtesy of Ron Starkey

effectively shattered last weekend when I joined the others of Dad's Army for the Father and Son Camp.

There must have been some wry fatherly smiles when this week's fun page in the 'Westmorland Gazette' reported that 'sons gave fathers some friendly help' and failed to add 'at most times – except when cooking and washing up were in the offing'.

The camp began on a lovely summer Friday evening and we were immediately impressed by the superb choice of site just above Red Bank with its views over Grasmere Lake and the Fairfield fells. We were impressed, too, by the excellent organisation which had taken place before our arrival. The main tent was up and equipment for each Patrol was ready grouped. Patrol Leaders (Scouts) knew where Antelopes, Buffalos and Cheetahs were to set up their tents.

All fathers were relieved to discover that Scouts had gone modern in cooking and that Gaz replaced rubbing two Scouts together to generate heat!

Details of our weekend activities will probably be dealt with elsewhere so I merely want to record how admiringly fathers viewed the range of activities offered. The careful planning and preparation that ensured the success of each item was impressive and, to my knowledge, nothing misfired from start to finish. Each item was presented to us as a challenge and in a way that invited enthusiastic participation – as far as ageing bones and flesh could manage!

The orienteering showed us the need for clear thinking, accurate map interpretation and a trust in the direction indicated by the compass. We still haven't discovered whether the team heading over the Scottish border on a back-bearing was led by a dad or a Scout!

The initiative tests were challenging and amusing. It was sad to see the entire Cheetah Patrol wiped out by an exploding wicker basket almost at its moment of triumph and the less said, the better about Antelope's inability to light a fire in twenty minutes. Just a further word of thanks for Gaz is all that is needed, I suppose.

Wives, you should have been there to see your husbands bearing a strange device festooned with bells and hellish cans of acid. So stalwart were they, so involved, so dedicated, so very British in all they did, that not one sound of complaint did they utter – in fact, apart from one muffled curse from an unnamed Patrol (Scout? Dad?) not a sound was heard! You would have been proud, indeed!

When 'Night Games' were first mentioned, I pricked up my ears. A recent visit to the library had led me to Mai Zetterling's somewhat risqué book of that name and I thought that progress from fire to Gaz was admirable and reasonable, but this

Top: Working off energy with giant push ball on loan from Westmorland County Youth Service.

Left: 1st Kendal tug of war team at County Scout Sports R to L: Adam Burgess, Andy Banks, Lawrence Bates, David Jackson, Mark Laurie.

was going a bit too far, even for today's permissive society. However, my innocence was preserved, for the 'Night Games' were dark versions of the Wide Games I remember from my own Scouting days.

There are so many memories of a very full weekend that keep flooding back – the 25 foot flag pole made from Scout staves and string, the delicious smell of bacon drifting over the site, the stories told late at night!

This Father and Son Challenge Camp provided us with an opportunity to experience a Scout camp at first hand. It allowed us to work side by side with our lads in a variety of situations. It created for us the opportunity for simple companionship, so difficult in the modern bustling world and only possible in the 'back to nature' situation in which we found ourselves.

But above all, we came away full of gratitude for the dedicated work of all the Scouters. We left feeling privileged that our boys were in the hands of a devoted group of men. We saw at close hand the enormous amount of hard work entailed in running a Scout Troop, and we saw too, that the 1st Kendal Scouters carried out their duties with imagination, with enthusiasm and with skill.

From all the fathers, a heartfelt thank-you, not only for the excellently organised camp, but for the week by week pleasure and experience you give our lads.

P.S. I feel it should be widely known that Antelopes were the winning patrol. We richly deserved the honour. At one time we dads didn't think we would make it, but through patience and a helping hand, we managed to cover up the faults of the Queen's Scout* in our midst and enabled him to share with us the success of the patrol!

'Little Aynam News', May/June 1969.

* The Queen's Scout mentioned was Roger Downing, who was a stand-in dad for a relative. Roger later became Scout Leader of 1st Kendal Troop.

Cartoon drawn by Ken Hughes

The Westmorland Gazette van that transported us everywhere at weekends. L/R: Bill Duff, Clarry Walker, Roger Downing (behind), Geoff Waterworth, Mike Sagar, Bruce Cowperthwaite, Alan Baker, David Goff and Jim.

Chapter Ten

Troop Transport

How fortunate we Kendalians are to live so close to the Lake District with all it has to offer! However, back in the early days of the 1st Kendal when so few people owned a car, getting there was difficult. Our problem was solved in an unlikely way by Vincent Mayor, the managing director of the Westmorland Gazette. It was Mr. Mayor who generously allowed us to use the newspaper's delivery van at weekends, subject to Clarry being the driver. This bright yellow two ton Commer van could be seen in the most unlikely place in the Lake District, and Tarn Hows became its second home. In 1954 the 'yellow peril' conveyed our racing car, its driver and pit crew to the finals of the soap box derby races at Scarborough, after Cub Scout David Parker had previously won the North-West regional event at Morecambe. I remember being stopped when crossing Scawton Moor by an alert policeman wondering what a Westmorland Gazette van was doing in Yorkshire.

In 1959 we purchased a green, ex Civil Defence ambulance from Westmorland County Council for £25. Syd Turney and I fitted it out with bench seats, and it served our needs until a better ambulance became available also for the princely sum of £25. The green ambulance was sold to Andy Murphy, Kendal's genial Irish scrap dealer for £25! Our new white Bedford ambulance was the type seen on 'Heartbeat'. It had a powerful six-cylinder engine and would climb even the steepest hills with ease. I fitted it with two comfortable leather seats from Mr. Murphy's magical yard (I was sometimes called Skip 'Steptoe' Cannon), and driving the vehicle was a delight. It proved thoroughly reliable and gave us freedom to attend many events, including Gang Shows at Carlisle, air displays at R.A.F. Anthorne, the Welsh Jamboree at Brecon Beacon and Barbon Sprint Hill Climb for cars. On that occasion I turned down a request by the organisers for the use of the ambulance in the event of an accident.

Some journeys were not without incident. Carrying canoes on top of an ambulance without a roof rack is difficult. On these occasions we would rest our canoes on inflated wagon inner tubes and secure them to the ambulance with rope fore and aft. One day on our way home, just as we left the dual carriageway at Ratherheath, one of the inner tubes worked loose and I watched in horror as it hit the road and bowled off downhill towards

Winner of the regional Soap Box Derby. The winning driver, David Parker, is on the right and David Goff is seated in the car. Also in the picture are Bruce Cowperthwaite and one unidentified Scout. The car was made on a wooden chassis and was fitted with three-speed Sturmey Archer gears. Under the rules the total cost was not to exceed £7.10.0d.
David came fourth in the finals held at Scarborough.

Our £65 Austin minibus driven by Syd Turney crossing the moors en route to Ardnamurchan.
Madge Turney is driving the Triumph Herald behind.

traffic travelling in the opposite direction. It hit the front of a car, bouncing over its bonnet and roof before coming to rest against a wall. The Rev. E. E. Oliver, Vicar of Staveley, was the startled driver and I am grateful to this day that he magnanimously forgave me the error of my ways.

At the best our ambulance would do about 20 miles to the gallon and I remember running out of petrol on Victoria Bridge in Kendal. Half a dozen Scouts pushed it halfway along Sandes Avenue to Raven Park's garage. His petrol pump was a work of art. It involved hand-pumping fuel up into an elevated, graduated, clear glass container. Then, with the nozzle secure in the vehicle's tank, he would reach up to open a valve which allowed the fuel to flow from the container to the vehicle by gravity. His garage was subsequently demolished to make way for Blackhall Road, and I hope that this early part of motoring history was kept somewhere safe for posterity.

In 1966 we bought an Austin minibus from the cricket club at the Provincial Insurance Company for £65 and our ambulance departed for Mr. Murphy's scrap yard to become his office. 'To be sure, Jim, it's grand for catching the b.....s pinching me stuff. With the darkened glass I can see out, but they can't see me in here.'

Even though it was a big vehicle, most of the Leaders felt comfortable driving the Austin and it was in use most weekends. One memorable trip was Easter 1963 when we were on our way to spend eight days at Camas Inas on Ardnamurchan. Going through Glencoe, we ran into a ferocious blizzard. Syd was driving the minibus which was loaded to the hilt with eleven passengers inside and some of our gear plus two canoes on the roof, making it fairly unsteady. He could barely keep it on the road and when the wind forced him to stop, the vehicle was almost blown over.

Our Easter camps on Ardnamurchan were not without transport mishaps. Syd and Madge Turney had fallen in love with this remote part of Argyll and had holidayed there many times, staying at Camas Inas. This place was little more than a long field on which were sited the owner's home, a former shepherd's cottage, and three static caravans, but its location on the edge of Loch Sunart made it special. Syd and Madge had explored Ardnamurchan and found it full of interest: at Fascadale a salmon fishing station where in the old days caves packed with winter ice would serve as a huge refrigerator, a ranch owned by Boot's the Chemist breeding Highland cattle and a village complete with school, built by the Forestry Commission to house its workers and their children. A favourite place for me and many of the boys

Terry Howarth's Ford Zodiac being loaded with camp equipment. Note the lack of roof rack.

Canoe trailers made by Andrew Kelly and Geoff Bainbridge and our Sherpa minibus at Fellfoot.

was the lighthouse, because the keepers allowed us to be present when they were lighting up and they found time to explain how everything worked. This lighthouse, incidentally, marks the most westerly point on the British mainland.

It was from Camas Inas, using the caravans as a base, that our Senior Scouts would set out in Patrols on four day expeditions as part of their training to become Queen's Scouts. In those days, before mobile telephones, I would try to visit each of the three Patrols during the second day to check on their progress and to make sure that all was well. In 1963 I had hired a go-anywhere Land Rover to carry our equipment and in this Ken, Barbara and I, together with David Atkinson who was about to become a Leader, set off on our visits. After successfully catching up with two Patrols, we continued to look for the third. They were some distance away and after studying the map I decided to take a shortcut on a green road over the moors. All went well until we hit ice over soft ground. However, by engaging four-wheel drive we continued on our merry way. But not for long! Soon the road became a bog and with all four wheels spinning, we found ourselves well and truly stuck. In fading light David Atkinson and I set off to seek help, leaving Ken and Barbara to try to keep warm in the stranded vehicle. Some distance on we came to an isolated farm and I noticed an old Ferguson tractor in the yard. Could that be the solution to our problem? A lady answered my knock and I quickly explained our predicament. 'I'm afraid my husband's down in the village cutting hair, but I'll ring around to get him to come home. You wait back at the Land Rover and he'll be there before long.' After a long time, during which it started to snow, we heard the welcome sound of a tractor. 'Let's see what we can do,' said our saviour as he attached an old piece of rope to the stricken Land Rover. Under tension it snapped almost immediately and after two more unsuccessful attempts, he set off back to the farm to find a chain. By this time the cold and the snow were getting us down and not one of us was practising what was asked of us in Scout Law number eight, which we had all solemnly promised to keep. You will recall that it demands that 'a Scout smiles and whistles under all difficulties.' Much to our delight the farmer soon returned, but our optimism was to be short lived. With the chain attached we stood and watched as the almost bald tyres on the old tractor skidded round and round and the Land Rover stayed put. After asking where we were staying, the farmer said he would get help from the nearby sawmill in the morning. In the meantime he would arrange for a taxi to take us back to Camas Inas. 'Just walk down the lane to the road and wait by the telephone box. It's not far and the taxi will be there soon.' It may not have been far, but trudging through the snow which was now falling heavily, it seemed like miles! Once at the kiosk, Barbara, Ken and I huddled together inside, leaving poor David out in the cold no doubt wishing he was with the lads, who by now would be snuggled up in their tents! Half an hour later the taxi, a Morris Traveller, arrived. Cold and miserable, but looking forward to getting warm and to a hot cup of tea – or perhaps something stronger – we arrived back at the shepherd's cottage to find that the generator had been shut down for the night, leaving us in total darkness and unable to make a hot drink!

The next day, just as the farmer had said they would, the men from the sawmill turned up and, with some considerable difficulty, using a huge tractor equipped with a winch and two big prongs, they managed to get the Land Rover back on its wheels! Without going into detail about the operation I can tell you that it involved pulling it on to its side, using the winch. I was surprised and very relieved to find that the soft bog had saved it from damage. I was still slightly worried about the charge for their labour, but when I asked they said, 'Since you are with the Scouts, there'll be no charge!' I believe I gave them ten pounds to share which, combined with the bottle of whisky for the farmer, seemed a very cheap price to pay! This was one of those incidents I would rather forget, but Barbara never let me. If I had a pound for every time she reminded me of that cold huddle in the telephone booth, I would be a wealthy man!

Kendal's well-known coach operator F. W. Stainton and Sons was our preferred choice of transport to summer camps. This firm, which has occupied its present site on Burton Road since its formation in 1921, started out as general engineers and haulage contractors. Using a stripped out, open topped charabanc they would haul all manner of goods during the week. Come the weekend it would be thoroughly cleaned and, with its seats refitted, Kendalians dressed in their Sunday best would enjoy trips around the Lake District. Our driver for the summer camps was always Frank Wright, who when he retired in the 1990s had worked part-time for the company for 56 years. He was a good friend and supporter of the 1st Kendal. Sometimes we had the luxury of retaining Frank's services - and the bus - for the duration of the camp. At Marlow on the Thames this enabled us to visit Windsor and London where we would always visit the Science Museum during the day and in the evening take in the Royal Tournament at Earl's Court. I recall one Marlow camp when one of our first time campers was terribly homesick. The Leaders tried really hard to help the poor lad, but nothing seemed to work. When he went missing, it triggered off a huge search and you can imagine our relief when he was eventually found sitting in Frank's coach drinking tea and watching T.V. We continued to involve him in activities throughout the camp, but his only solace that week came from frequent visits to Frank in the bus.

After many years good service the Austin became very unreliable, and in the summer of 1970 the Group decided to aim high and replace it with a brand new, twelve seater Land Rover at a cost of nearly £1000. Raising that amount of money was a huge undertaking. We kicked off with a twenty mile sponsored walk, planned for the 20th September, and boys were issued with cards well in advance and told to get busy collecting sponsors. Stuart Mawson, one of six excellent boys from the Milnthorpe/Storth area in the 1st Kendal, plucked up courage and, card in hand, rang the bell at Dallam Tower, the home of Brigadier Tryon-Wilson. The Brigadier answered the door himself and after Stuart had explained the purpose of his visit, he replied, 'Well done! How does a pound a mile sound?' In those days when 6d (2½p) a mile was generous, it sounded very good indeed! The Brigadier was Vice President of the Westmorland County Scout Association and well known for his charitable work in the community. Eighty people completed the walk in continuous rain and raised about £400 – a great start! On the 8th December a cheese and wine evening to celebrate the arrival of the new vehicle was held for all who had helped make the purchase possible.

It was a good vehicle on short journeys, but driving it on long motorway trips I found it noisy, uncomfortable and slow. On one journey to Henley–on–Thames, towing a trailer loaded with canoes and faced by a strong head wind, it averaged eleven miles to the gallon and struggled to make sixty miles an hour even on downhill slopes. I ached for days after each of these long trips.

Throughout the 1970s collecting waste paper was a good fundraiser. When we heard that the Freshwater Biological Association had a load of waste paper at their headquarters on the west side of Windermere, Bill Clarkson, our Group Secretary, and his two Scout sons, Simon and Jonathan, set off to collect it with the Land Rover. They enjoyed their ferry ride across the lake and were soon hard at it loading the paper. In no time at all they were back on the ferry enjoying their second ferry ride of the day, this time with the Land Rover loaded to the roof. On arriving at the Bowness side of the lake, however, the Land Rover refused to start. It was too heavy to push and with no means of getting help, they found themselves heading back across the lake again! To cut a long story short, the three Clarksons spent two hours toing and froing across the lake! Bill was very grateful to the man in charge of the ferry for his tolerance, though towards the end he did say, 'If this goes on much longer, I am going to have to charge you!' Perhaps it was hearing this threat that made the stricken vehicle decide to start, as it miraculously did in the end!

There have been three other vehicles since those days, some more comfortable than others. One, a red Sherpa, which is over 20 years old, can still be seen conveying a former Group Treasurer, joiner George Thorpe, and the tools of his trade around town.

Currently boys in 1st Kendal travel in comfort in a 15-seat deluxe minibus, safely held in by their seatbelts, but I doubt whether they have the same fun and excitement as our Scouts from fifty years ago roughing it in the back of the Westmorland Gazette van.

Chapter Eleven

Take to the Boats!

For an adult to pursue memorable childhood activities without appearing eccentric is difficult. All is not lost, though. Any Scoutmaster worth his mettle can easily relive those happy occasions of long ago by introducing the same activities into his Troop meetings. In Natland, where I grew up, a large pond would appear in one of the outlying fields after periods of prolonged rainfall. Its arrival would create new opportunities for us children. In winter the frozen pond would see us rooting out our sledges and whooping with joy as we headed off for hours of unbridled fun. It was here that I took my first shaky steps on rummage sale skates strapped to a pair of old soccer boots. Since then, right up to my early sixties, I can hardly recall a winter when I didn't enjoy outdoor skating.

Summer time ponds presented different but equally exciting things to do. Swimming was the main activity, but for my ten year old pal Geoff George and me, our thoughts focused on ship building. With four oil drums, a few boards, some binder twine, assorted nails and a hammer we beavered away and worked wonders. Egged on by the promise of 'a go', there was no shortage of young helpers when the time came to transport the craft to the pond. The launching was seldom achieved without one of the oil drums breaking free. In those days, before I had joined the Scouts and learned to do lashings, getting round drums to stay put was a major problem. Eventually, armed with my mother's clothes prop, we would cast off for high adventure. We nearly always returned home wet through, but thoroughly happy.

Coincidentally, my last rafting experience also took place on that flooded field in Natland. Well into retirement, I was pleased when Natland lads Nye Jayne and David Causey, both Scouts in the 1st Kendal, called at my home to seek help with building a raft for *the* pond. It was good to know that something I enjoyed more than sixty years ago still appealed to boys of today.

When I became Scout Leader with the 1st Kendal, I felt it almost a duty to share the delights of raft building with my Scouts. In the 1950s commercial size inner tubes were more readily available; polystyrene and plastic had arrived and raft building became that much easier. One Sunday during the summer of 1956, Clarry and I together with Bill Duff and John Barber loaded up my little van with raft building equipment and a small Anzani outboard engine and headed for Windermere. Our mission: to build a motorised raft! As we set about the task we were encouraged by a small

Early raft with outboard engine on Windermere. Crew: John Barber and Bill Duff.

group of well-wishers with words like 'Grand lads the Scouts!' It's at this point if you remove 'Bill and John' that the comments would more likely be 'Look at those strange men behaving childishly!' With the raft complete, the engine fuelled and life jackets securely in place, John and Bill set forth on proving trials. Nothing dropped off, the engine performed well and, when they returned to land, I was beginning to think of the possibility of creating an entry in the Guinness Book of Records for the first powered raft crossing of Windermere. However, shortly after leaving for the second time, the intrepid pair were halted by the Lake Warden and escorted back to shore. John recalls the warden saying, 'It spoils the look of the lake, boys!' I am sure his concern must have been for their safety and that he must have thought it too dangerous a place for two lads to be out on a raft, but that was not the way he came across to John who still remembers the incident well!

In 1936 Great Tower, a 250 acre plot of wild countryside on the eastern side of Windermere, was presented to the Boy Scout Movement for camping by Mr. W. B. Wakefield. It became a place where Scouts could test their backwoods skills and hone up on camping techniques. Back in 1961 three thousand Scouts from different parts of the country camped there at a charge of 6d. (2½p) each per night. Although the site did not extend to the lake, access to the shore was available through the kindness of a local lady, Mrs. Spellers of Moor Cragg, who also allowed Scouts the use of a large boathouse. It was here that Mac Smith, the Bailiff of Great Tower, allowed us to spend weekends out of season. In the 1950s, along with Margaret Hall, I had learned how to sail at Brathay Hall's excellent centre for outdoor pursuits on the north-west corner of Windermere. At that time my only road transport was a D.M.W. trials motorbike, and to get us there I borrowed my brother's Panther motorbike complete with sidecar. I had never ridden one before – or since – and I am sure the same goes for Margaret in the sidecar. To this day I marvel that Ralph let me have it without hesitation.

One Friday night at the end of October, Clarry, six lads and I arrived at the Moor Cragg boat house and settled in. The next morning we awoke to a dull but dry day with fresh winds. After a hearty breakfast we rigged one of the 18 ft. wooden boats and with me at the helm and Clarry, Bill Duff and Bruce Cowperthwaite as crew, we set sail. The other lads had opted to use the second boat for rowing practice. Out on the lake we made good speed and quickly found ourselves close to the western shore. When the wind strengthened and became blustery, I decided it was time to head back to the shelter of our boat house. A sudden squall and an involuntary gybe in the middle of the lake and over we went! We clung on tightly to the gunwale of the rocking boat as white tops began to crest the waves. In the middle of the trauma, Bill's concern focused on his gabardine mac which was

Streamlined raft paddled by Charles Longden and Philip Herd

The Eden raft race at Carlisle.

floating away. 'Me mac, me mac! Me mother will kill me!' Thankfully Bruce was able to grab it just in time! The lake, which had been dotted with craft when we set out, was now completely empty. Conditions as they were prevented the other Scouts from coming to our rescue, so there was little we could do but wait and hope! Thankfully, two workmen, repairing the roof of a lakeside cottage, had watched the drama unfold and had telephoned for help, before somehow managing to locate a rowing boat with oars and come to our rescue. Back at the boathouse we changed into dry clothing and sat in front of a warm fire, which the other boys had prepared, and almost immediately the police, a doctor and the ambulance men arrived! After making sure that we were unharmed, they took our personal details and left. Embarrassingly, the following Friday the Westmorland Gazette carried a full report about the incident, the saving grace for me being that they wrongly labelled Clarry as the responsible Scout Leader and me as his assistant. After fifty years I had hoped that this incident would have been totally forgotten so it was with some consternation that, a year ago while reading the Gazette, I spotted the report again under the heading 'From Our Files: 50 Years Ago'!

For many years raft building was an integral part of summer camps held near water. Tarn Hows was another popular venue and a huge number of rafts were built here by Cubs, Scouts and their Leaders. From the land near our hut the nearby island was a popular destination. Capsizes were a common occurrence and were enjoyed by spectators on the mainland. It was all the sweeter if the person in the water just happened to be a Leader!

On the River Kent opposite the old gunpowder works below Sedgwick, I recall a group of us building a raft and Bruce Cowperthwaite piloting it down to the footbridge before being hoisted on the end of a rope by willing hands from above – a rescue mission without a helicopter! (see p66)

For many years Kendal Youth Council ran raft races on the Kent from the Lads' Club at Beezon Place, where Home Base is now, down to Abbott Hall Park. They would attract as many as twenty rafts from a variety of youth clubs within the town. The Le Mans start across the river was always spectacular and often resulted in early retirements. Over the years we tried many different designs. On several occasions Trevor Hughes and Peter Laycock had success with a raft built on buoyancy bags reputedly from Wellington bombers. Another of our rafts, constructed from two hospital air beds wrapped in canvas and suspended under a wooden frame, was also a winner with Mike Anderson at the helm.

When Cumbria was created in 1974, county raft races were held on the Eden at Appleby and later at Carlisle. All sorts of innovative ideas came into

Le Mans start of raft race, near Victoria Bridge.

Wednesday night training session on Windermere. For many years our canoes were built and maintained by my friend Norman Stilling.
L to R: Trevor Hughes, Scott Pearson, Ben Allen, Paul Stelfox, Nick Allen, Chris Lowe, Lawrence Bates, Yvonne Laurie.

play and some exciting races took place in the nearly twenty years that we took part. In these bigger races 1st Kendal boys won many trophies, often cheered on by their families who made a day of it and enjoyed a picnic by the river. One or two mothers have been known to run along on the riverbank shouting encouragement to their sons!

Bob Meakin's corgi enjoying a ride on my £15 canoe.

On warm summer days during my childhood whole families of Natlanders, armed with picnics and rugs, would head off for a quiet stretch of the River Kent just north of Robin Hood Island. The sound of children's laughter would ring out as we splashed and swam in the slow-flowing water. We would frequently find ourselves sharing the water with cows quenching their thirst on the other side of the river. On one occasion a young man in a red canoe or – technically speaking - kayak expertly negotiated our swimming pool and I watched longingly as it disappeared out of sight downstream. I vowed that one day I would do the same, but it would be 1954 before I achieved it. That year I bought a brand new canoe. It was 15 ft. long and constructed from a wooden frame sheathed in canvas. It cost £15 including delivery from the builder in Gloucester to Oxenholme Station! With my brother's help I carried it down to the half-filled canal below Natland. I found it easy to paddle and knew this activity would prove popular with the Scouts.

When Leslie Somervell, a member of the K Shoe Somervells, gave us a two-seater German 'Faltboot' (a folding, rubber-skinned canoe) that had once crossed the English Channel, a lot of Scouts got a chance to sample canoeing. Our trips were not without mishaps. I recall one trip with John Barber, Bruce Cowperthaite and Alan Baker where, after satisfactorily negotiating the River Kent through Kendal, we arrived at Scrogg's Weir near

Watercrook. It had been built to provide waterpower for Gawith's, one of Kendal's old snuff works. With soft-skinned boats the weir called for portaging. John and I were soon able to climb aboard and continue our journey, leaving Alan and Bruce some way behind. As we rounded a bend we were confronted with overhanging, low branches and capsized. We managed to grab hold of the canoe and scrambled ashore. As I stood on the bank, I watched with horror as the two in the second craft suffered the same fate. Our predicament called for action, and as we were only a mile from my home, I decided we should head there to dry out. About an hour later I was able to deliver to their homes three dry boys kitted out in some of my old clothes.

The need for more canoes for the Group became urgent as more and more boys wanted to take up the activity, and in 1961 I attended a canoe building course at Kendal's Technical College. Armed with this knowledge, a group of Scouts, Ken Hughes and I set about building our own canoes. We worked hard throughout the winter and by the next spring we had a fleet of ten canoes, a prodigious output from a bunch of amateurs!

Canoes are difficult to transport, but Peter Fell, the blacksmith at North Western Gas Board, designed and built us a trailer to carry seven boats. It was easy to tow and immediately made our lakes and rivers accessible. The sheltered bay at Pull Wyke on the northwest side of Windermere with its speed restriction of 10 mph, even in those days, became our favourite venue. It was here that countless Kendal Scouts got their first taste of paddling a canoe. Over the years we canoed on Ullswater, Rydal Water, Grasmere, Esthwaite Water and Tarn Hows, as well as on the rivers Lune and Brathay, not forgetting the Kent which was literally on the doorstep of our headquarters. I recall transporting canoes to Coniston Water to enable us to see Bluebird, only two weeks before Donald Campbell's fatal attempt to break the world water speed record.

In the 1960s the introduction of fibreglass revolutionised canoe building. With the use of a mould, a light, durable canoe, capable of withstanding knocks on river journeys, could be built quickly and relatively cheaply. For a while I thought we had wasted our time building ten canvas canoes, but when we offered eight for sale to parents, they sold like hot cakes. Some of the money received enabled us to buy four brand new fibreglass canoes, and soon after Westmorland County Scout Council chipped in with six more on condition that they were made available for other Scout Groups to use under my supervision. With the balance of the money I bought two light touring canoes constructed from thin beech plywood and fibreglass. They had been purchased by Manchester Education Committee for use at their Tower Wood Outdoor Pursuit Centre where they had been deemed too unstable for beginners.

Be prepared to get wet! Canoe tug of war at Aldwark.

Throughout the 1960s Eskdale Outward Bound School sponsored a canoe race for young people over a seven mile course from Fell Foot at the south end of Windermere northwards around Grass Holm Island and back. It was called the John Chase Trophy Race in memory of a former canoe instructor at the school. It was here, in 1966, that we made our first nervous entry into the world of canoe racing. The following year six members of the Group took part in two single seat, and two double seat canoes and I reported the event in our 'Little Aynam Newsletter' at the time: 'In a southerly gale the competitors battled with huge waves made worse by maniacs in speedboats and the canoes were soon out of sight. After rounding the island, most of the competitors, sensibly, took to the shelter of the shore, but Trevor Hughes pressed on doggedly with decks awash to win in 1 hr. 25 mins. Anne Powell, a Young Leader with our Cub Pack, came a creditable fourth and our two doubles teams of Peter Laycock and Mike Murphy, Brian Wilson and Michael Nelson came second and sixth.'

In 1968 we received an invitation to compete in the inaugural canoe race for Scouts over the ten and a half mile length of Windermere. It attracted a hundred canoes for the four events, two for singles and two for doubles. You can imagine my delight when we came away with two firsts, Brian Wilson winning the singles event for 14 to 16 year olds in 2 hrs. 1 min. and Peter Laycock the 17 to 20 year old event in 1 hr. 54 min. The race in 1970

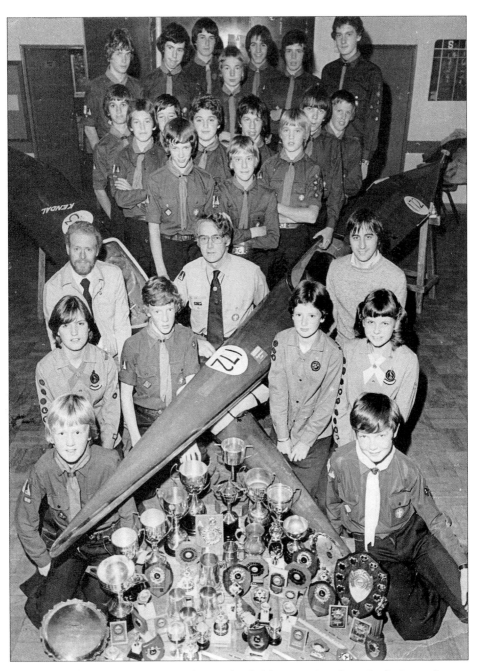

Canoeing trophies won in 1978. Front: Chris Head and Philip Goss. Second row: Sandra Lecore, Stuart Mawson, Julie Ellwood and Anne Lacey. Third row: Trevor Hughes, Jim Cannon and Geoff Bainbridge. Fourth row: Mark Nicholson and (?). Fifth row: Michael Wilson, Dan Anstee, Ralph Horsley, Simon Clarkson, (?), Steve Head and Andrew Clement, (?). Back row: Philip Talbot, Simon Horsley, Jonathan Lacey, David Lecore, (?), David Ellwood and Graham Starkey. Courtesy Westmorland Gazette was worthy of note and the 'Little Aynam News' carried the following report at the time:

WINDERMERE LONG DISTANCE CANOE RACE

13th September, 1970

Since its introduction just three years ago, the ten and a half mile Windermere Long Distance Race has become popular. Races are held for Scouts (14 and 15 years) and Venture Scouts (16 – 20 years) using single and double seat canoes. The variety of canoes in use these days is such that to provide fair competition the able organisers from S.E. Lancashire arrange no fewer than nine separate class events. With an entry of over two hundred, the planning is formidable.

Having built a couple of touring doubles during July and August we had the necessary canoes to enter all nine classes but, as most of our boys are unable to manage the unstable racing double, we settled for eight.

Training sessions were held over sections of the course three times a week during the preceding month and records kept of individual times. As the 13th drew near everyone, bar Richard Tallon who had dislocated an elbow playing soccer, was in good shape and capable of producing a good time.

Anyone interested in unusual transport could do worse than visit Waterhead car park on race day. This year's models ranged from a five ton builder's lorry carrying two canoes through a variety of ex War Department petrol gobblers to an Austin 1300 with seven canoes on tow and two on top. Thank goodness our Land Rover has arrived at last! The atmosphere is carnival but competitive.

At 9 a.m. prompt the Scout slalom and touring singles were 'klaxoned' away. Our lads, Andrew Nelson and Geoff Bainbridge, were amongst the leaders as they disappeared from view beyond the steamer pier.

Next to go were the Scout racers (Phil Sharpe) and the double tourers (Mike Anderson and Rodney Woodhouse). Then the Venture singles slalom (Brian Wilson) and tourers (Peter Laycock – winner in 1968), followed fifteen minutes later by the Venture touring doubles (Nigel Byrom and Clifford Williams). By the time the final class, Venture Racers (Clive Ormandy) departed, the first class had been on the water for 40 minutes and the leaders were approaching Belle Isle.

From various vantage points along the lake spectators watched with interest. Near the Beech Hill Hotel we could see another Scout slightly ahead of Andrew Nelson and the rest behind spread out over a huge area. We could see Brian and Peter overtaking the Scout competitors at a great rate of knots. At Fell Foot, in brilliant sunshine, we waited anxiously as two specks appeared on the horizon. They were neck and neck with 400 yards to go when Andrew pulled ahead with a fine burst of speed to win in 2 hrs. 1min.

Canoes arrived thick and fast. The staggered start made winners difficult to spot, but we felt we had done well. As the last 1st Kendal canoeists arrived, they were cosseted by our excellent service team of Laycock, Tunstall and Sharpe – fathers of Peter, Chris and Phil - who provided coffee and lifted their canoes out of the water. Soon the waiting was over and our hopes confirmed. We had won eight classes out of eight and established records in seven!

This was the last Windermere race I was able to fully enjoy as I took over the organising from then on. I have lost count of the sleepless nights I spent worrying about the weather, safety precautions and logistics. After a few years we had it down to a fine art with all the Leaders in 1st Kendal taking on jobs, and eventually responsibility for the organising went to Geoff Bainbridge who by then had become a Leader.

During the next decade there was a huge growth in the number of Scouts taking up canoeing and new races sprang up all over the northwest of England. River races were held on the Ribble at Clitheroe, the Dee at Chester and the Weaver near Runcorn whilst other races took place on canals at Wigan, Daresbury, Ormskirk and Forton. A further event was held on Rudyard Lake near Congleton. Former 1st Kendal Scouts Geoff Bainbridge and Andrew Kelly built us an excellent four-wheeled trailer to carry fifteen canoes and this enabled us to compete in all eight events. In one year Scouts from the 1st Kendal won 50 trophies! Buoyed by our successes we journeyed to Buckinghamshire, with a little apprehension, to compete in a race from Henley to Marlow. On this occasion we stayed overnight at Maidenhead Grammar School where Len Reynolds had become Headmaster. We were pleased when we returned home having won some of the races. It was almost worth the pain that I endured the following week from driving our Land Rover the 500 mile return trip! Participating in this race became an annual event and our success continued.

For a number of years we also took part in a unique forty mile race on the Leeds Liverpool Canal, spread over two days. Teams of three would tackle this event and paddlers could be changed at any time. The two who were not paddling at the time were required to keep in touch with the progress of their paddler, as they were needed to help with portaging at the many locks.

In 1967 Ken Hughes, Trevor and I travelled to Lancaster Baths to learn the Eskimo Roll and armed with this skill, we ran classes for our Scouts in

Kendal Grammar School Baths. In later years Geoff Bainbridge and Trevor Hughes repeated the training and took over running the classes at the swimming pool at Troutbeck Bridge.

We visited the Scout Association's Water Activity Centre at Marlow to camp or take part in races. It was here that I had my first paddle in a K4, a four-seater 36 ft. long racing kayak made in Struer, Denmark. It had been used by the British team at the 1960 Rome Olympics. It was beautifully made from laminated wood, and I looked at it longingly on every visit. Years later when we were able to buy it, I recall four of us Leaders setting out one Saturday in our Land Rover, equipped with a very long V-bar, to bring it home. It overhung the Land Rover by about ten feet either end, which caused a lot of interest. At a red light we were behind a Mini and watched as the driver jumped when the front end of a kayak suddenly appeared above and in front of her. It was not a practical craft, but it gave us a great deal of pleasure paddling it on Windermere. It now takes pride of place on a wall in the Steamboat Museum near Bowness.

After almost thirty years canoe racing came to a halt. The association's insistence on Leaders being qualified through the British Canoe Union was a contributing factor in their demise, but I think it was more that the races had simply run their course. It gives me pleasure to know that some of my former Scouts, among them Geoff Bainbridge and Andrew Kelly, continued with the activity long after the Scout races had been discontinued. Andrew, especially, distinguished himself and reached the top division in B.C.U. racing.

It is sad to see that of the seven Kendal firms represented on the gateway at the Lakeland Jamboree, only two now remain in business: Romney's Mint Cake and Gawith's Snuff Manufacturers.

Chapter Twelve

Jamborees

In 1957 I was privileged and not a little surprised to be chosen to lead a sixteen strong contingent of Scouts representing Westmorland at the World Jubilee Jamboree at Sutton Park in Warwickshire. The Jamboree also celebrated the centenary of Baden-Powell.

The contrast between my first inauspicious camp with twelve boys on a sodden lakeside 'hay meadow' and being part of a camp for 25,000 boys from 84 countries on a 350 acre site (the area of 175 football pitches) could hardly be greater. Sutton Park itself covered three and a half square miles.

The word jamboree was chosen by B.-P. for the first international gathering of Scouts at Olympia in 1920. The dictionary defines it as 'a celebration of merrymaking' and I think it is an excellent choice. 'Jamboree' is now known and understood all over the world.

The Scouts chosen to represent Westmorland came from Grasmere, Windermere, Arnside, Heversham, Milnthorpe and Kendal. The representatives of 1st Kendal were Bruce Cowperthwaite, Mike Molloy and Geoff Waterworth. We met a few times to get to know each other and to discuss logistics for going to the Jamboree. On the 30th July the lads travelled by train with their personal equipment, leaving me to take care of all the camping gear. I had recently bought my first brand new vehicle, a 5 cwt. Ford van which I had fitted with a roof rack – and ocelot seat covers!! It cost exactly £350!

Finding the Jamboree was easy as there were AA signs everywhere. At the main gate I was immediately struck by a huge archway supporting a large globe and by the vastness of the camp. Tents and marquees seemed to stretch as far as the eye could see. A helpful camp policeman directed me to site number 52 in Arrowe Park sub-camp which was just over a mile away. As I drove slowly down Jubilee Way, I passed the camp hospital, consisting of four long tents arranged like the spokes of a wheel with the hub being a green lawn, complete with flowerbeds. I hoped that we would not have need of this facility, but it was good to know it was there. An ornamental gateway marked the entrance to the five sub-camps each bearing the name of a previous Jamboree. To reach the Arrowe Park sub-camp, you had to pass through the Copenhagen sub-camp whose gateway was a very impressive life size replica of a Viking ship, supported high up on timber scaffolding. There was so much to see it was difficult to take it all in.

They arrive from everywhere. (Jamboree Journal, Sutton Coldfield 1957)

When I eventually reached our campsite, which, over the next ten days, we Westmerians would share with 16 Scouts from East Cheshire, I received a warm welcome. In no time at all, I was given a mug of tea and a piece of cake by their Leader while his Scouts set about unloading my van. A good start! When, over an hour later, the Westmorland boys arrived, we all set to with a will and soon had our tents up and a good kitchen prepared complete with an altar fire. This raised fireplace safeguards the grass and allows the cooks to do their job from a standing position. After tea we took a wander around our sub–camp to meet some of our fellow campers. In Arrowe Park sub-camp thirty-one nationalities were represented. Our immediate neighbours were from Barbados and Cuba, followed by Taiwan, Costa Rica, Armenia, Canada, South Africa, Sweden etc., a wonderful mix of languages, uniforms and colourful characters.

The organization of the infrastructure in this 'city of tents' was impressive. Everything 25,000 people could possibly need for ten days of living together was provided. 25 miles of water mains had been laid, special Jamboree stamps were available, the fire service was on hand, the B.B.C. had a broadcasting Centre set up etc. In addition to the five sub-camps, there were two more set slightly apart. One was called Moot, an old Anglo-Saxon word for a gathering of the clans, and held Rover Scouts (young men aged 18 - 24) from twenty-four different countries. The other was called Indaba, a South African word for a gathering of native tribes, and was for leaders who were attending without any boys in tow.

Supplying food for 25,000 men and boys must have been a huge undertaking. At the end of the ten days, the Jamboree newspaper reported that we had consumed: 54 miles of sausage, half a million eggs, 1,125 gallons of soup, 72,000 gallons of tea and coffee, 2,250 sacks of potatoes, 16,000 pounds of tomatoes, and 3,200 packets of breakfast cereal. Each Troop was given tokens to exchange at the quartermaster's store for our daily food rations.

The Camp Centre provided many of the features associated with a town of 25,000 and it was the main meeting place for Scouts and visitors alike. Here were shops, a theatre, the camp newspaper print shop, the B.B.C. and the World Press, restaurants, cafés, public lavatories, lost property office, police and fire stations, and a post office. To enable overseas Scouts and visitors to understand British industry, an 'Industrial Pavilion' housed a wide range of finished products, and in some cases work was actually going on making certain articles. The exhibits ranged from steel production, locomotive building and ship building to the making of brushes, just to name a few. There was even a demonstration of one of Birmingham's oldest crafts, gun making, showing in detail the process involved in the manufacture of sporting and other types of guns!

1912: B.-P. married Miss Olave St. Clair Soames, later to become World Chief Guide. The car was the wedding present given by his Scouts, who subscribed one penny each.

The Rolls Royce and caravan presented to Lord Baden-Powell in 1929 and bought with a penny gift from each Scout.

In the Baden-Powell Pavilion, an exhibition of personal trophies, treasures, photographs and many other interesting items including B.-P.'s Rolls Royce and caravan could be seen. In 1929, to mark the 21st anniversary of the Scout Movement, every British Scout contributed one penny to buy a present for Lord Baden Powell. Lady B.-P. was asked to find out what he would like without disclosing the purpose of the enquiry, and the only thing the Chief Scout could think of was a pair of braces. His wish was fulfilled - with the addition of the car and caravan!

Our unique National Health Service was showcased in another marquee alongside an exhibition emphasising the need to safeguard nature and our national resources. The PYE T.V. Centre marquee was a great attraction. Here boys were able see themselves on television screens, a novelty for all at that time, but especially for the boys from third world countries who had never seen a television before. Other attractions included underwater television cameras and a complete range of radios and televisions.

The day after our arrival 20,000 of us packed the vast camp arena for the opening of the Jamboree by the Duke of Gloucester, the President of the Boy Scout Association. In the huge stands overlooking the ground T.V. cameramen with their enormous, cumbersome cameras and sound commentators relayed the whole ceremony to all parts of the world. The flags of all 84 countries represented at the Jamboree were paraded as our Master of Ceremony outlined some of the great events in Scouting history: the Siege of Mafeking, where B.-P. got the idea for the Movement, the first camp at Brownsea Island, the first Jamboree at Olympia etc. At 3 p.m. the Duke arrived accompanied by Lord Rowallan, the Chief Scout of the British Empire, and General Sir Rob Lockhart, our Camp Chief. A warm U.K. welcome was extended to all the overseas Scouts who, after the Jamboree, would receive hospitality with British families before returning home. The Duke of Gloucester reminded us that each one of us lucky enough to be at the camp represented 200 other Scouts in the Movement. At the conclusion of his speech, a maroon flare was fired, and the flags of every participating nation were broken from the masts outside the arena. He left to three rousing cheers and later took time to visit each of the five sub-camps.

On the third day, the Jamboree buzzed with excitement in anticipation of the visit of the Queen and Prince Philip. From an early hour thousands of visitors poured into the camp, and by the time the royal party was ready to begin their tour, the dusty roads of the camp, were lined with campers and visitors several deep. Inside the arena, in brilliant sunshine, the Cresswell Colliery Band played to the waiting crowds and at 3 p.m. the Queen, followed by Prince Philip, entered the royal box. The national anthem was played followed almost immediately by the March Past. Where possible, 24

Queen Elizabeth II and Prince Philip giving us a wave as they drive past our campsite while touring the Jubilee Jamboree in 1957.

The Westmorland Contingent at the Golden Jubilee Jamboree at Sutton Coldfield, 1957. Unfortunately, I can only identify half the contingent: Peter Hildrew from Grasmere, Ian Bowman and John Mallinson from Windermere Sea Scouts, Jim Mitchell from Arnside, Jack Cordukes from Milnthorpe and Mike Molloy, Bruce Cowperthwaite and me from 1st Kendal.

Scouts from each country in the camp took part. They were led by Aden, followed by Armenia, Australia, Austria etc. until all had passed before the Queen. As the last strains of the music died away, the arena filled with Air Scouts who put on an impressive display, culminating in two Scout-piloted gliders landing in the arena. The royal party then left in an open top Land Rover to start a tour of the five sub-camps. There was much to see and admire and, even for the well travelled Queen, the number of countries visited in a day must have been a record. At the Moisson camp, the Queen and the Duke were introduced to the leader of the Iran contingent. Here Scouts dressed in national dress performed the 'chouchani', an Iranian folk dance. Before moving on the Royal couple saw an exhibition of Iranian handicraft. Now, almost fifty years on, a beaten copper plate bearing the Iranian Scout Badge and inscriptions in Persian adorns the wall of the lounge in my home. This treasured souvenir of the Jamboree is a constant reminder of happier times when there were Scouts in Iran.

At the Finnish camp a cookery demonstration was put on, and after the Queen finished her tour, some of the Scouts were seen to cut out pieces of the turf she had walked on for souvenirs. A calypso band greeted the Royals at the Jamaican camp where they saw a meal of banana fritters being cooked. As the Queen left to continue the tour, the band played 'Take her to Jamaica where the rum comes from.' Wherever she went, the Queen, who had been a Patrol Leader in the Girl Guides and a Sea Ranger, received a warm welcome. Half-way through the tour the royal couple had tea in one of the central marquees, and here she was introduced to the Leader and the youngest Scout from each contingent. A rare honour for a privileged few! Westmorland must not have been a 'contingent' of sufficient size to be included, as I did not receive an invitation.

The tour continued and when much later our honoured guests departed they left us with lots of good memories. How many people can claim that they received a smile from the Queen and Prince Philip as they drove past their front gate?

In the middle of the camp, 30,000 Cubs arrived with their mums, dads and Leaders for a good day out at the Jamboree. Hundreds of chartered coaches and 23 special trains brought boys from all parts of the country, including Kendal. Bill Bagley, Assistant Leader with the 1st Kendal, brought some of our boys. I was particularly pleased that two of my Senior Scouts, Alan Baker and John Barber, came along. Some had started their journeys at a very early hour, knowing that it would be late before they arrived home. The main activity of the day was the arena show where a thousand Cubs entertained us with a pageant entitled 'The Circus Comes to Town'. To turn out so many boys in such immaculate costumes, heralds in red, green and blue, soldiers, clowns, acrobats, sailors and even elephants, zebras, penguins and chimpanzees, must have involved many hundreds of mothers and thousands of hours of work. After a fanfare from some gold and red heralds, we saw a grand parade of all the performers led by the 'massed band', well over a hundred strong. These were followed by the acrobats, sailors, chimps, clowns, hobby-horses and spacemen, who all formed up into a tableau at the back of the arena. Three armies then beat the Toy Town Tattoo and performed the changing of the guard. They finished with a very noisy mock battle. The acrobats arrived to give us a show of gymnastics and this was followed by the animals of the circus who performed various tricks including a football match between the elephants and the zebras. Then, steaming over the horizon, came S.S. Wolf Cub manned by sailors and accompanied by dozens more sailors. We were treated to some hornpipe dancing and finally 'GREETINGS TO THE SCOUTS OF THE WORLD' was flagged up in semaphore. No sooner had the ship departed than spaceships arrived, accompanied by spacemen. We were treated to a 'space dance' to music from Gustav Holst's Planet Suite. At the end of the show a thousand Cubs shouted out their motto, 'WE'LL DO OUR BEST'.

Every day we were spoilt for choice of things to do and it was often difficult to choose. The arena events included displays by the Royal Canadian Mounted Police, music by a 175 strong band from the United States which included boys from every state, the Army Motorcycle Team and folk dancing from many nations. On the Sunday thousands of Scouts gathered to join in community hymn singing. Because of the many religions represented (the U.S. alone brought five chaplains: one Protestant, one Roman Catholic, one Rabbi and two Mormons), services were held in different areas of the camp. The main service in the arena was led by the Archbishop of York.

A lot of time was spent in entertaining casual visitors, who dropped by to have a chat and to exchange badges, and in visiting other sites to the same purpose. The exchange of badges is a very big thing at international Jamborees, and many Scouts take extra hats and belts along for trading. One day the Westmorland boys were invited to have tea with the Scouts from Ceylon. We were told that their ornate entrance gateway was similar to the decorative arches outside royal palaces and Buddhist temples in their country. There was a display of local art and crafts for us to see before the tea was served, Ceylon's best of course. Songs from Ceylon followed and when the folk dancing began I was easily persuaded to join in. In Strictly Come Dancing terms I probably rated a one! It was a fun afternoon and as a thank-you we left gifts of Kendal Mint Cake. I never thought that now, fifty years on, I would be watching Ceylon – now Sri Lanka – on the television giving England a lesson in how to play cricket.

Most evenings Scouts from around the world put on a show for us in the Camp Theatre. To get a ticket you had to be there early in the day, but it was well worth the effort. Where else would you be able to see Irish dancing followed by hand bell ringers from Birmingham? Jamaica's contribution included the Banana Boat Song, acted out by the singers, and a Calypso Pole Dance. Canada entertained us with a square dance with some fine 'girls' as partners. An interlude of piano music by a talented Leicester Scout was followed by songs and madrigals by the Filipino contingent. Then Rhodesia gave us two songs and a Zulu dance before the Scottish contingent closed the evening with some reels and pipe music. Each night the whole audience left the theatre singing the Jamboree Song which had been written for the occasion by Ralph Reader. I still remember the words:

March, march, march on the road with me,
To the Boy Scout Jamboree,
Join the throng and swing along
As we sing our song:

Chorus:
Jamboree! (clap, clap), Jamboree! (clap, clap)
Come give three hearty cheers,
And we'll march along together
Another fifty years.

Ev'ry hour let the valleys ring,
With the scouty songs we sing,
Underneath the stars at night
In the camp fire's light.
(Chorus)

We're the boys of the left-hand shake,
Boy Scouts all and wide awake,
Hiking over hill and dale,
Singing on the trail.
(Chorus)

Marching on with the B.-P. lead,
Every colour, every creed,
All for one and life is good,
In our Brotherhood.
(Chorus)

Years from now down a mem'ry lane,
We shall walk and live again
These great days with you and me
At the Jamboree!

When Lady Baden-Powell, World Chief Guide, finally brought the Jamboree to a close, it was a fitting end to a memorable occasion. Before returning home, many of the overseas Scouts would enjoy home hospitality with British families.

Ten years later Stephen Evans from Casterton, Peter Laycock from 1st Kendal and I were America-bound. The three of us had been chosen to represent Westmorland at the 12th World Jamboree at Farragut State Park, Idaho. Another big surprise for me! The site chosen was on the wooded shores of Lake Pend Oreille and as this was America's first World Jamboree, we knew it would contain some surprises. In preparation for sharing a campsite with boys from Yorkshire, we had spent a few weekends camping with them to get to know them.

The daily routine was similar to the Sutton Coldfield Jamboree, but some of the events were very different. At one of the campfires we watched in amazement as a space-suited 'astronaut' with rockets strapped to his back performed a vertical take-off, made a few circles above the arena, hovered for some time above us, before landing back on the spot from which he had taken off. The whole spectacle was made even more impressive by a spotlight being trained on him throughout. Perhaps it would not impress youth of today to the same degree, but in 1967 it was like watching something out of a science fiction movie!

On another occasion Vice President Hubert Humphrey dropped by to tell us how much he had enjoyed being a Scout, although he had never made Eagle Scout, the highest award in America. I could have told him that Harold Wilson, Prime Minister at the time, had also been in the Scouts, but he had made King's Scout!

Each day, in the centre of the Jamboree, a huge Skill-O-Rama provided a showcase for presenting national Scout crafts. I took a daily interest in the building of a birch bark canoe by three American boys and their leader. The finished object was quite beautiful. I would have loved to have paddled it on Windermere.

A memorable event was when a fleet of yellow school buses conveyed several thousands of us to a rodeo ground some distance away. Here we were treated to a traditional western rodeo put on by professionals who do nothing but follow the annual rodeo circuit. Although I had a pretty good idea what to expect, I was impressed by the daring of the cowboys. They performed everything from bare back riding to steer wrestling, bull riding to calf roping and bronco riding to chuckwagon racing. Throughout the performance there was a real sense of excitement and danger. Perhaps the most dangerous task was carried out by men dressed as clowns, whose job it was to divert the attention from the cowboy who had been thrown by the bull or bronco, while he limped or was stretchered from the arena. Having more or less mastered simple techniques in lasso spinning, and knowing how difficult it was, I was extremely impressed by the skills shown by some of the cowboys. After the show the 'feeding of the five thousand' took place in an adjacent field, but not by a loaf and two fishes! This being ranch country, we were confronted with enormous amounts of beef which had been cooked in great big pieces in a very long trench. It must have been in the ground for hours as it was very tender and tasty.

Although I met many interesting and very nice people at both major Jamborees, I cannot say that I formed any lasting friendships at either of them, but while in America I did meet some people who would become life long friends. They were the family I stayed with after the camp, when home hospitality was offered to all us foreign campers. A group of us from Westmorland, Lancashire and Yorkshire flew to Salt Lake City, Utah, where we were to spend the next nine days as guests in people's homes. Along with Simon Bromley, a dentist's son from Lancashire, I was welcomed into the home of Eldon Johnson, an elder in the Mormon Church, and his wife Metta. They were the perfect hosts, taking us on trips into the mountains, sailing on Utah Lake, and around to the homes of their friends so we could learn more about life in the Western States. They even took us along to a family reunion where I was asked to say a few words and answer questions about 'the old country'. One question was whether English teenagers, like their American counterparts, drove cars, and I think I shocked them when I answered that they had to settle for bicycles and small motor scooters as petrol was much too expensive in England! Several years later I was able to repay some of their kindness when they came to stay with my mother and me for a week, and we continued to correspond until Eldon's death in the early nineties.

I was not the only one to have been treated royally by my hosts. Peter Laycock was actually taken on a trip to the Grand Canyon – an amazing experience for a lad of about eighteen!

Although very few have the opportunity to attend a World Jamboree, all of the Scouts in the 1st Kendal during the 1960s were able to enjoy international camping by attending smaller, regional Jamborees in this country. These gatherings were more affordable and attracted a good mix of Scouts from here and abroad.

I have good memories of Jamborees which we attended in Wales, Warwickshire and Devon. Unbelievably, in 1960 the chosen site for the

Ian Shepherd presenting Chief Scout, Sir Charles Maclean with Kendal Mint Cake.

The 1960 Lakeland Jamboree campsite at Calder Hall, now Sellafield

Lakeland Jamboree was Calder Bridge, where our view was dominated by Calder Hall Atomic Energy Establishment, now Sellafield. Today some parents and Leaders might object to such a location, but in those days we were unconcerned and had a very good camp.

When we returned from the Welsh Jamboree in August 1961, I wrote the following report to the Westmorland Gazette:

Seventeen members of the 1st Kendal B Scout Troop, under the leadership of Scoutmaster David Bone, arrived home on Saturday after spending ten memorable days at the Welsh Jamboree, Gwernyfed Park, Brecon. Scouts from twelve countries were among the 2,500 boys attending the Jamboree, and the guests at an international tea party, arranged by the Kendal Group, included Scouts from Canada, Ireland, Greece, Wales, Southern Rhodesia and Scotland.

The Kendal campsite, which contained many novel features, included a fireplace constructed from an old blacksmith's forge. A rustic gateway, adorned with plaques displaying some of the main industries of the town, attracted great interest. Sir Charles Maclean, Chief Scout of the Commonwealth, who spent a day at the Jamboree, and Lord Kenyon, the Camp Chief, expressed pleasure at being presented with Kendal Mint Cake by Maurice Black and Charles Waddington.

During the camp various qualifying tests for the Queen's Scout Badge, including a rugged 50 mile explorer hike and a canoe journey down the River Wye, were undertaken by three senior Scouts from the Group. In the competitive events the Troop won the 'Jack Blunt Disguise' competition and was adjudged the third best campsite in the Jamboree. An impressive international camp-fire brought the Jamboree to a close. The Kendal Group is proposing to visit Powers Court, near Dublin, for the summer camp next year.'

It was not the only time Sir Charles Maclean was to be presented with Kendal Mint Cake. It happened again at the Devon Jamboree in 1964 and the presenter was the Troop Leader, Peter Laycock. In addition, he was also given a sample of the 'famous' Natland Treacle, the presentation made by a Natland boy, Eldred Himsworth. The gateway was an improved version of the one used in Wales and was adjudged one of the best in the Jamboree and was shown on B.B.C. Southern Television.

Charcoal cooking was an innovation at the camp and, in spite of very wet weather during the first three days, some excellent meals were prepared, including, according to the newspaper account, a dinner of roast chicken, sage and onion stuffing, green peas and roast potatoes!

This Jamboree was of similar size to the previous one and had campers from Iceland, Libya, Iran, America, Nigeria and most European countries as well

1st Kendal and 1st Kendal Rural Scouts at the 1964 Devon Jamboree. Front row: J. Nelson, M. Crorie, M. Powell. Second row: J. Rawlinson, M. Williams, P. Laycock, B. Elshaw, C. Walker, J. Cannon, K. Hughes, D. Bone, D. Cutt, E. Himsworth, C. Waddington, T. Swainbank. Third row: M. Nelson, B. Bainbridge, E. Bond, L. Thompson, W. Procter, T. Molloy, C. Ormandy, D. Riding, M. Conway, J. Stobbart, P. Briggs, A. Blair, D. Greenbank. Back row: P. Greenbank, H. Park, P. Cheeseman, C. Harper and P. Reynolds.

as all parts of the United Kingdom. Throughout the Jamboree many friendships were formed. On one day Charles Waddington and his Patrol were invited to tea by the Libyan Scouts, while on another, the Icelandic Scouts enjoyed coffee at the Westmorland camp and sampled snuff to a chorus of sneezing!

Devon International Jamboree, 1964. Fox Patrol 1st Kendal Rural Troop, winners of the Camp Gadget Trophy: Maurice Williams, Bill Bond, Lewis Thompson, William Procter, Mike Nelson and Brian Bainbridge. 350 Patrols were in the competition.

The emphasis in the camp was on 'the Patrol' and in the 'Patrols in Action' competition the Fox Patrol of the Kendal Rural Troop finished first out of 350 patrols for campcraft and gadgetry. At the closing ceremony they were presented with a fine oak plaque and axe as prizes from the Camp Chief. Peter Laycock and Martin Crorrie also won a competition as members of a multinational patrol in the 'Operation Brotherhood' competition.

Leaders taking part were David Bone, Ken Hughes, Clarrie Walker and I, and Barbara Hughes was on the Camp Staff.

The following is a report published in the 'Little Aynam News' and written by Ian Harris, who was just one of several 1st Kendal Scouts to have been given the opportunity to attend a World Jamboree abroad.

11th WORLD JAMBOREE, 1963
MARATHON, GREECE

The 11th World Jamboree was held at Marathon, Greece, this year from 1st August to 11th August. I was fortunate enough to be chosen to represent Westmorland along with Bruce Wilkinson from Kirkby Lonsdale and Ian Richardson from Appleby. As there were only three of us, we were amalgamated with Scouts from the Durham and West Cumberland contingents, making up a Troop of 40, including 4 Scoutmasters.

The three of us left for Athens on the morning of Wednesday, 31st July aboard a B.O.A.C. Comet, and from Manchester the flight took only 3 hours 50 minutes at a speed of 520 m.p.h. and a height of 33,000 feet. Our route took us to the east of London, across the Channel, to the west of Paris, over the Alps, across Italy, down the Adriatic coast and then on to Greece.

On Thursday, 1st August at 7-30 p.m., Crown Prince Constantine, the Chief Scout of Greece, opened the Jamboree with a few words of welcome and then expressed his sorrow at the death of all the Philippine contingent in a flying accident.

The camp itself was huge, our particular campsite being about 2 miles from the main gateway and 1 mile from the arena. On Saturday we had a wide game in which every Scout had to make friends with 10 other Scouts, each being from a different country and a different sub-camp.

In a normal day we carried out normal camp duties such as cooking, washing-up, tidying and improving the campsite and making sure the fire bin was topped up with water, just in case of a fire.

We were very honoured on Wednesday, a week after leaving England, when Crown Prince Constantine visited our campsite. We were later told that he visited only 3 campsites in each of the 11 sub-camps. On Friday, Sir Charles Maclean also visited us, wearing shorts for the first time since his appointment as Chief Scout.

On Saturday, 10th August, we were allowed to go to Athens for a day and so all of us spent the day buying presents and souvenirs. At 5.30 we caught the bus back to the camp as the U.K. National Display was being held in the arena that night. The theme of the display was "Britain Gave the World..." and Durham contingent presented the Davy Lamp.

During the Jamboree Durham gained 100% in the Laurel Award and were awarded the Shield for the Best Troop in the sub-camp. Crown Prince Constantine closed the Jamboree on the Sunday night and wished us all the best in Scouting. He also announced that the next Jamboree was to be held in America in 1967.

On Tuesday, 13th August we started our four-day tour of Greece. We went first to Ossios Loukas, the monastery of St. Luke. It has two churches and is famous for its mosaics. Then on to Delphi, famous for its stadium, sculpture and the Spring of Castalia. We crossed the Gulf of Corinth from Itea to Aighion, stopping overnight in school rooms.

Next day we went to Olympia where we spent half a day looking around and spent the night at a German Red Cross Camp just outside Olympia. From Olympia we went to Tripolis, then on to Sparta and Mistra, Mistra formerly being a centre of Byzantine culture. Nauplia was next where we stopped the third night. Then on to Epidaurus, where there is the finest and most complete ancient theatre in Greece. After Epidaurus we went to Tiryns, Mycenae, Ancient Corinth and back to Athens.

As Bruce, Ian and I did not return to England until Sunday afternoon, we spent nearly two whole days looking around Athens, sleeping in a schoolroom in the outskirts of Athens. On Sunday afternoon we left Athens Airport at 6 p.m., 2 hours late and arrived in Manchester at 9.10 p.m., to be greeted with the usual English rain. While we were in Greece it rained for only 7 mins 50 secs - on the Saturday I was in Athens.

So ended a really exciting 3 weeks!

I. Harris, P.L. 1st Kendal Senior Scouts

Ian's enthusiasm and enjoyment are indisputable, and I must say that I also enjoyed the two World Jamborees I attended. However, having had the opportunity to reflect on all the Jamborees I attended, I have come to the conclusion that I prefer the smaller, international ones to World Jamborees, which are just too big. Like the Olympic Games, they have become prohibitively expensive, partly because each one has to be bigger and more spectacular than the last, thus excluding many countries from hosting them. I also doubt that they would get quite the same local and state government support today that the Sutton Coldfield Jamboree had. Just sending one or two boys to a World Jamboree can place a financial burden on a Scout Group and force it to spend a lot of time and effort on fund-raising just for that purpose. Stuart Davidson, who was a member of 4th Kendal before and during the war, attended a Jamboree in Moisson in France in 1948 which cost him £15. The fee for the Sutton Coldfield Jamboree was £15 and I paid £65 for the trip to America in 1967! In comparison, the World Jamboree in Thailand in 2003 cost each boy £2,500 which required a lot of fund-raising on behalf of the individual Scout, his family and the Group. It is also worth mentioning that the fee to attend the Centenary Jamboree, which is to be held in this country next summer (2007) is £895 for British Scouts - a rise well above inflation!

A proud moment. Jim with his first Queen's Scouts in 1959. Back row: Mike Allen, Mike Molloy, Bill Duff, John Barber. Front row: Bruce Cowperthwaite, Jim Cannon, Alan Baker.

Chapter Thirteen

Queen's Scouts

In 1909 King Edward VII conferred by Royal Warrant the award of King's Scout Badge as the highest achievement for a Boy Scout. When Queen Elizabeth II acceded to the throne, the badge was renamed the Queen's Scout Badge and in 1958 it became the Queen's Scout Award.

In 1946 Senior Scouts were established in this country with a programme of training relevant to boys 15 to 18 years old. Gaining the King's (Queen's) Scout Badge became the sole privilege of Senior Scouts. In the fifties and sixties it involved achieving challenges in several areas such as community involvement, adventurous activities and leadership. Proficiency badges had to be earned and to this end 1st Kendal received generous help from many quarters. St. John Ambulance and the Westmorland Fire Service were the mainstay of their public service training, but from time to time other professionals gave of their time.

The Senior Public Health Badge course, for example, was taught by Dr. Hampson, a young, married intern at Westmorland County Hospital, who had been a Scout at Clitheroe. In a series of lectures held in the library of Kendal Grammar School he dealt with the development of Public Health in this country and widened the subject to include human relationships, sexual health and relationships, the responsibilities of marriage and the implications of setting up a home. Nothing was taboo and all questions were answered in a straightforward manner. An examination at the end of the course resulted in a 100% pass which spoke volumes about the boys' interest in his talks. I recall that they clubbed together to buy him a framed Lake District water colour as a thank you.

The part involving leadership and public service called for providing practical help in the community over a sustained period. We agreed that this should be at least 36 hours. During the ten years that Clarry and I ran the Senior Troop, a wide range of 'good turns' were carried out, not always with success. We regularly found ourselves doing work for members of the Kendal Stick and Wheel Club, mostly concerned with gardening, and responding to requests from Mrs. Reegan, well-known champion of the old and needy. She involved us in all manner of tasks, including once moving a piano with our ambulance. We never questioned the authenticity of any requests, but very occasionally we were let down. I recall one occasion when Chris Tunstall, who went on to become a police inspector, was disgruntled – and rightly so – when he spent an afternoon digging the

The 1960 Queens Scouts: Anthony Clement, Barry Link, Roger Downing and Derek Marshall.

Ian Harris, David Cutt and Ian Ellison gained their Queen's Scout Award in 1962

garden for a handicapped lady, while her able-bodied twenty-something year old son just sat in the lounge watching T.V.

In my annual report for 1963, I wrote, 'At Whitsuntide some of the Seniors helped with the organisation and running of the Scout camp at Hawes Bridge and they laid on a splendid demonstration of tracking, camouflage and stalking as part of the Tracker Badge.

At the beginning of September ten Senior Scouts boarded our ambulance and set off to help run the County Patrol Camp at Lowther. Eldred Himsworth demonstrated the oral method of artificial respiration using a 'Resusci-Annie'.

Another suggested challenge was helping to run a Scout Troop, youth group or similar, and my Senior Scouts were given just such an opportunity in 1960. Sedgwick House, which had been the home of the Wakefield family (famous for pioneering the gunpowder industry in this country and much else), was taken over by Lancashire County Council after the war. It was made into a home for boys with epilepsy, many also with special educational needs. The Matron, Miss Sharpe, had approached Westmorland County Scout Council to ask if it would be possible to have a Troop for 'her' boys. Concern was expressed by our Field Commissioner, a professional within the Movement, who had doubts about the ability of some of the boys to understand the Law and Promise. However, the association gave the request its blessing and 1st Kendal Leaders, assisted by Senior Scouts, took on the running of the Troop on a rota basis. Bringing some happiness into the lives of these young boys each week was a highly rewarding experience and one that we all enjoyed.

As a part of their public service, twelve Senior Scouts undertook designing and building a gateway for the main entrance to Great Tower Scout Camp at Windermere. They came up with two huge, turreted towers, constructed from eight telegraph poles with a joining archway made from oak sourced from the Great Tower plantation. The lads spent many long weekends and evenings during the summer months of 1963 working on this project. From a newsletter at the time I see that the materials used included three dozen coach bolts and over 200 six inch nails! The whole thing was completed by the beginning of September, much to the delight of Mac Smith, the bailiff, and to the relief and satisfaction of the Senior Scouts. Were they to drive past there today, they would be pleased to see that the towers are still standing – 43 years later.

For many years we entertained the residents and staff at the Cheshire Home

The 1964 Queen's Scouts. Back row: Andrew Somes, Lance Porter, Alan Barker, Louis Baron, County Commissioner, Miss E. Reed, Mayor of Kendal, Jim Cannon, John Barber A.S.M., John Reed and Deryk Tebay. Front row: Eldred Himsworth, Ian Shepherd, Brian Elshaw, Keith Williams, David Atkinson, Martin Powell.

The last – so far – 1st Kendal Queen's Scouts, 1966. Standing: John Shaw, Mayor, Jim Hildrew, County Commissioner, Mike Murphy, Terry Swainbank, Kevin Turney and Charles Waddington. Seated: Alistair Craghill (4th Kendal), Trevor Hughes and Peter Laycock.

at Holehird with excerpts from our Christmas Gang Shows. It was something we all enjoyed. One year I received a very unusual request from the matron in connection with a forthcoming fund-raising day: 'Jim, we've been given a deer and it would be wonderful if you and your lads could spit roast it on the day to be sold as venison burgers.' During my years with Natland Scouts I had once – with moderate success – cooked a rabbit in clay, but that hardly qualified me for tackling a deer. With the enthusiasm of youth, I agreed. I could find no reference to spit roasting in any of my mother's cook books, not even Mrs. Beeton's, but undaunted and with a little help from Andy Murphy's scrap yard, we managed to build a functioning spit, complete with turning handle. When the great day arrived, we set off very early with a load of firewood, the spit and basting equipment. An hour after our arrival we had a substantial fire burning and set about the task of roasting the unfortunate, skewered beast. Thankfully, it was small and without antlers, skin or entrails! It was the start of six hours of very hot work! Our efforts provided good entertainment for a lot of people, but I'm afraid the end product could – at best – be described as a curate's egg. The matron thanked us most gracefully, but our culinary services were never called upon again!

To earn the Senior Explorer Badge, which was an obligatory element of becoming a Queen's Scout, Senior Scouts were required to undertake a fifty mile expedition over three nights and four days in unfamiliar and challenging country and to complete a log of the journey. Training had to take place beforehand in lightweight camping, map reading, compass work, accident precaution and expedition first aid. The first Scouts in 1st Kendal to tackle this journey were Mike Allen, John Barber, Bruce Cowperthwaite, Bill Duff and Bob Meakin. Because the test was being done in term time, they undertook a different hike on two consecutive weekends. The first one involved towing a trek cart, loaded with all their gear, from Kendal to the head of Longsleddale Valley and then over Sadgill into Kentmere Valley. After an overnight camp they continued over Garburn Pass into Troutbeck, a distance of 18 miles over the two days. Having recently read their joint log book, I am amazed and proud of what they achieved. Some of John Barber's comments written at the time give a good idea of the nature of the challenge:

Saturday:

2½ miles: We have just climbed a small hill and it has made us sweat and set us thinking about Sadgill where there is no tarmac and it is both steep and rough.

5 miles: Arrived at Garnet Bridge and thought about muffling the steel-rimmed wheels so that no-one would see us pass through.

The long haul up Garburn: Bob Meakin, Bruce Cowperthwaite, Bill Duff and Mike Alan.

7 miles: Two boys, not more than eight years old, volunteered to help us push the cart – every little helps. After we explained what we were doing and where we are going, one boy said that he thought we were collecting rags and scrap metal.

10 miles: Met farmer at Sadgill and after satisfying his curiosity, we set off up a very steep incline behind the farm. Began to rain. Conquered first hard piece after much pushing and pulling. Broke 10th Scout Law on the way [A Scout is clean in thought, word and deed].

11¾ miles: We've done it! Three hours after leaving Sadgill. All this time has been spent pushing, pulling and dragging the cart and digging up rocks. We keep falling over stones and on the slippery grass. How we managed it without injury, I'll never know!

13 miles: Arrived at Kentmere, pitched tents and got busy lighting a fire and cooking a meal: soup, stew, bread and jam, and coffee. Decided to have an early night.

Sunday:

Woke up to find farm dog munching our breakfast bacon. Cold morning. Couldn't fry eggs as we had no bacon fat. Porridge burned, so we had to settle for boiled eggs, bread and jam. Having paid the farmer, we struck camp and left with his words ringing in our ears, 'There's a motorbike trial over Garburn today'. The track is extremely rough and it is difficult to keep moving. To make progress we are having to set ourselves a series of targets to reach before we have a rest. Often we don't make it and are forced to stop, puffing and panting. Just met first motorbike in the trial. The rider shouted out, 'Crikey, I thought we were mad!'

We are nearing the top now and the ground is getting boggy. With the wheels sinking in the mud making progress is difficult. We finally reached the top (1,500 ft.), almost too tired to continue, but after that pull it is not surprising. Whilst we are eating our dinner, the motorcyclists start returning, this time calling out, 'How the hell did you make it?'

We begin the journey downwards. The track is rough with deep ruts and we manage to stop the cart with difficulty. After an eventful journey, we garage the cart at Holehird and head off for a café at Windermere for a well-earned drink and a rest.

The following weekend the boys bussed to Coniston and set off on the second part of the test over Coniston Old Man (2,631 ft.), then on to Seathwaite Tarn to explore the disused mines. After reaching the road between Ulpha and Wrynose Pass, they crossed the River Duddon and set off on the long walk to Ulpha. Next they followed the track around Stickle Pike (1,231 ft.) and on to Dry Hall Farm before picking up the road to Torver. It was dark by the time Torver was reached and the tents erected. Next morning at Torver Common Wood the boys inflated a rubber dinghy, which Syd and I had left there together with a canoe. They crossed Coniston Water with the canoe towing the dinghy and landed at the far side by Fir Island. They then had to find the fire tower on High Man (923 ft.) and from there continue to Hawkshead. This was actually the journey's end, but as there was no Scout van waiting for them, they had to walk an extra five miles to catch the ferry and cross to Bowness to get a bus home.

On the 15th October 1959, Mike Allen, Alan Baker, John Barber, Bill Duff, Bruce Cowperthwaite and Mike Molloy received their Queen's Scout Badges from Mr. Hornyold-Strickland, Lord Lieutenant of Westmorland, at a special ceremony held in the Council Chamber at the County Hall in Kendal. Later in the year they travelled to London to receive their Queen's Certificates from the Chief Scout, Sir Charles MacLean, at a ceremony in the Goldsmiths' Hall. These were high points, not just in the lives of the lads, but in the history of the 1st Kendal.

Another successful attempt at the trek cart challenge took place in 1959, this time starting from Troutbeck. Three of the team, Roger Downing, Barry

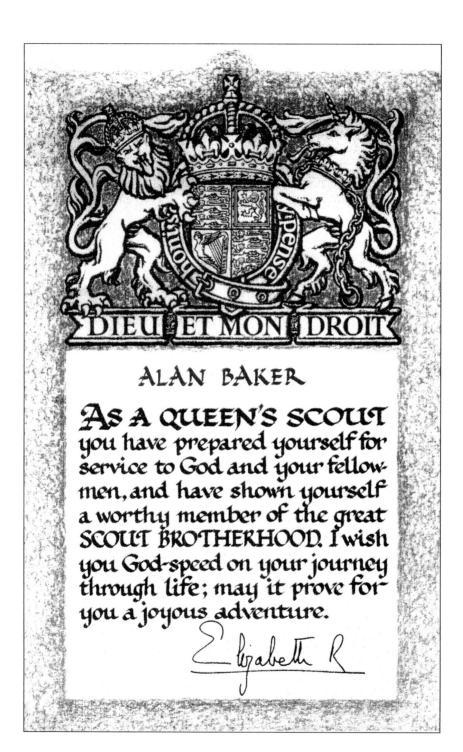

Alan Baker's Queen's Scout Certificate.

Link and Derek Marshall, together with Anthony Clement who chose to hike instead, went on to receive Queen's Scout Awards from the Chief Scout at a reception held at Colston Hall, Bristol. Before returning home, they enjoyed a tour of Sir Peter Scott's Wildfowl Centre at Slimbridge. Roger Dangerfield, who had completed the trek cart challenge with them, was unfortunately confronted with an orthopaedic problem which required extended hospital treatment. This deprived him of the opportunity of becoming a Queen's Scout.

David Cutt was our next Queen's Scout. He was the 'clerk of works' for the gate building project. A proud Scot, how pleased he was to receive his award from Mac Smith, a fellow Scot and the bailiff at Great Tower Scout Camp!

From November 1962, in response to a request from our County Commissioner, I wrote Scouting C.V.s for all of our Queen's Scouts to be read out during the presentation ceremonies. Looking through them now, I am again reminded of what a splendid bunch of lads they were, and I have drawn out some of the comments I made about them to give the reader an idea of the calibre of these boys. Obviously, many comments refer to their Scouting prowess: '...is a likable, gentlemanly Senior, who has always done his best for the Group and has developed into a first class leader,' '... quickly endeared himself to his Scoutmaster with his industry, good manners and proficiency with the tea pot', and 'As a Gang Show Stalwart, his parts have ranged from boy soprano to village policeman. He has even cheerfully taken on female roles.'

However, the lads had many interests other than Scouts: canoeing, sailing, skiing, playing the guitar, photography, stamp collecting and working for the Red Cross, to name a few. One lad even held a private pilot's licence, and a couple owned and maintained their own motorbikes! I am also reminded that not everyone got through their years in 1st Kendal without the odd scratch and even a broken bone; one boy ended up in hospital in Fort William with a damaged knee and another, who became known for his willingness to test all sorts of pioneering projects, paid for the honour with a cut scalp, a soaking in the Kent and a few minor injuries.

In addition to the Queen's Scout Award, the following 1st Kendal Senior Scouts also gained the Gold Standard of the Duke of Edinburgh Award Scheme through Scouting: John Barber, Bill Duff, Bruce Cowperthwaite, Eldred Himsworth, Peter Laycock, Keith Williams, Ian Ellison and Mike Molloy.

*The Equerry-in-Waiting to The Duke of Edinburgh
is desired by His Royal Highness to invite*

Mr. John Barber

*to attend the presentation of Awards to boys and girls who have
reached the Gold Standard in His Royal Highness's Award Scheme,
at the Palace of Holyroodhouse
at* 10.30 a.m. *on* 28ᵗʰ June 1961

*A reply is requested to
The Equerry-in-Waiting to The Duke of Edinburgh,
Buckingham Palace, S.W.1.*

Dress: Lounge Suit.

P.T.O.

Please bring this card with you.

John Barber's Invitation to Presentation Ceremony.

For the names of all thirty-one Queen's Scouts, please see the captions under the photographs.

In 1967 Clarry retired from Scouting and when a District Venture Scout unit was started a couple of years later, I reverted back to my old job of running the Scout section. We both agreed that the ten years we had spent running the Senior Scouts had been some of the best years of our lives. It was a privilege to have worked with these very fine lads.

Chapter Fourteen

Viva España!

Terry, Clarry and I became good friends and often socialised on a Sunday evening. Sometimes we would drive to the Drunken Duck at Outgate for a drink and a plate of freshly made sandwiches. I remember these sandwiches fondly, because the landlady, Mrs. Barnes, made them especially for us even though they were not on the menu and her husband didn't want her to do it. I suppose he was worried that it would set a precedent.

Other times we would go to Morecambe to see a show at the Winter Gardens. They attracted some very big names in those days and put on fantastic shows. I remember going to see Ted Heath and his Band, David Whitfield, and the high-kicking Tiller Girls. On the way home we would stop off at Bolton-le-Sands for supper at a little café. It was on one of these occasions that we came up with an idea to take some of the older Senior Scouts camping to Spain. Clarry, being a married man with family responsibilities, gave the idea his blessing, although he wouldn't be able to go himself.

When we aired the idea at the next meeting, the boys in question were immediately up for it, so now there was no backing out! I wrote a letter to the Youth Department of the Spanish government in Madrid, asking if they could direct us to a campsite on the shores of the Mediterranean. I added that it would be a bonus if we could share the site with some Spanish boys. I was aware that since General Franco came to power there weren't any Scouts in Spain, but I did not know that the National Youth Movement existed; it was run very much on the same principles as Scouting. In my naivety, I went ahead and made all the arrangements for the trip, unaware that the application to go abroad should have been channelled through Scout Headquarters in London, so I was relieved when retrospective permission was granted.

The next thing I had to do was arrange the transport. We needed a vehicle that could take eight men with their personal gear as well as all the camping gear. I managed to hire a Commer 'dormobile' with a pop-up roof from R. Smith & Son in Windermere. The pop-up roof made it possible to stand up inside, but it also meant that we didn't have a roof rack, so the inside was packed to the very limit.

Because my memory is not nearly as good as his, I have asked one of the 'boys', Alan Baker, to write the report on the trip:

In 1960, before the days of package holidays and timeshares; when only the wealthy or the members of the forces travelled abroad, a group of eight Senior Scouts set off on a grand adventure by dormobile to Spain.

Waiting at the docks at Dover; Terry Howarth, Jim, John Barber, Barry Link, Alan Baker, Mike Sagar, Bob Meakin, Bill Duff.

With Jim and Terry Howarth as drivers, we left Kendal and travelled down to Dover for the ferry crossing (and of course this was also before the days of motorways). Remembering most of the time to drive on the wrong side of the road, we made our way through northern France, and were amazed to find ourselves being greeted with enthusiasm by the people in all the towns and villages we passed through. Then it dawned on us that, in our Scout uniforms (visible only from the waist up), and with a sign on the front of the vehicle proclaiming '1st Kendal Scout Troop' and the fleur-de-lys, they obviously thought we were some remnant of the liberating troops returning for a post-war event.

We travelled through Troyes, Chalons-sur Saone, and down the Rhone valley, camping en route, except at Chalons, where a kindly hotelier offered to accommodate us in his posh hotel at an unbelievably low price. We crossed the border into Spain and passed through Gerona and on to our destination at the resort of Blanes on the Costa Brava. Today it is a modern resort with high-rise hotels and all the trappings of package holidays – then, it was a small coastal village with a souvenir shop and a couple of bars.

Our campsite was in a sandy wooded area near the beach, which we shared with the 'Falange Juventud' – a very nationalistic uniformed youth movement. The trees were festooned with loud-speakers from which martial music was played, and twice a day, they paraded to a shrine where some ceremony was performed – as none of us spoke Spanish, a lot of it passed over our heads, but we were made very welcome, and were made an offer which we were able to refuse. They kindly invited us to share in their eating arrangements, but after the first meal, which consisted of a thin gruel containing bits of gristle and other unknown, but vile-tasting ingredients, we decided that we would rather go hungry. Whether as a result of this first introduction to Spanish camp cooking, or our own food preparation, it was not long before we began to take it in turns to go down with the dreaded 'gippy tummy'. The suffering was made all the worse by the primitive sanitary arrangements – a series of holes in the ground surrounded by an adobe wall, bearing in large letters the distinctive word 'latrinas'.

During our stay in Blanes, we went off on trips into the hills to visit many intriguing mountain villages, where conditions were so primitive compared to our sophisticated Kendalian upbringing – whole communities with unmade roads, no power or running water – it made us realise how privileged we were. In one village, where we wanted to buy milk, the whole village turned out to bring us a cow to milk, and then to have a communal guided tour of our dormobile and its facilities. An orderly but excited queue formed and all had to be shown how the roof went up and down, the taps ran with water (until it ran out) and the gas rings went on and off. Their water supply was provided by a scrawny old nag that walked round a windlass all day to pump water from a deep well.

Horse walking around a windlass drawing water from a well in Spain, 1960.

We did, to our discomfort, go to a bull-fight, taking our seats with the locals on the scorched sunny side of the bullring (the cheap seats). Having endured the whole 'corrida', we were disturbed by the cruelty of the event to the bull and the poor horses.

And of course, we swam, and sunbathed, and got burned, and bought lots of cheap souvenirs to bring home.

After a week at Blanes, we set off on our return journey towards Andorra, which we reached via a twisty, climbing dusty road. Eventually, at the customs post, we were detained for a long time, during which we were entertained by the Spanish customs people lining up a bus-load of peasants along the wall, while they systematically stripped the bus of its seats and radiator. We stayed only two nights on a campsite in Andorra, where the showers (hooray, luxury at last) were fed by water straight from the snow-clad peaks (brrrr!).

Our journey then took us over the mountain passes of the Pyrenees, where we had to make frequent stops as the engine kept boiling over. This was probably the most exciting part of our travelling, as the roads were steeper and twistier and more hair-raising than anything we had expected. But the views were absolutely spectacular.

On the return journey through France, we camped overnight on a site on the banks of the River Lot in Cahors. During the night, there was the most horrendous storm, and when we woke in the morning (those who slept), the river was half-way up the campsite and just short of our tents. A far cry from the unaccustomed heat we had been getting in Spain.

Our last night abroad was spent camping in an old gun emplacement in the sand dunes near Le Touquet. Taking our last francs and centimes into a local café, the proprietor watched us counting our money like a gaggle of trainee misers, and realising our poverty, gave us each an extra egg with our fried egg and chips. Travel certainly broadens the mind – it obviously taught us not to trust foreign food, but to appreciate their kindness.

On arriving at Dover the following day, we had been advised that it would help the customs people if we had a list of our purchases ready to hand. So we wrote the whole lot out on a toilet roll, which we fed out of the window to the jolly customs officer. 'Ho, ho', he said, 'very funny. Clear off!' Welcome home.

To a group of teenage lads, used to the quiet rural civilisation of Kendal, the whole experience was quite an eye-opener. Everywhere we were treated with kindness (except by the motorcycle gendarme who fined us ten francs for speeding) and made most welcome. We were introduced to all the funny ways of foreigners – driving on the right, eating strange food, enjoying hot weather, having siestas, armed police and militia, bizarre sanitary arrangements, talking very fast. It was all very un-British; it often required displays of initiative when situations arose which we were completely unprepared for; and it gave us a wonderful insight into ways of life and travel, which are now so commonplace.

In 1965 Terry and I and another group of Senior Scouts set forth to seek further adventure in sunny Spain. This time we had observed the correct procedures and the Delegacion Nacional de Juventudes had provided us with an excellent campsite at La Escala (Gerona). We shared the site with thirty Spanish boys, all from the same village, who were cared for by the village headmaster, the parish priest and the local doctor. They also had trained catering staff to provide their meals. It was a big change from the basic facilities from our earlier visit to Blanes. Although we operated our camp independently, the set-up provided huge benefits for us, not least that we were able to buy our food cheaply through them. The Spanish boys had horses at their disposal and allowed us to use them also. When I say 'us', I must admit that owing to another rather painful experience, previously mentioned, with horseback riding, I didn't actually take advantage of this offer, but the boys enjoyed them. When confronted with the chargers, they learned that they came in two varieties: 'lento' and 'rapido', and one or two of our boys bravely chose 'rapido'.

One day our hosts invited us to join them on a specially chartered boat across the Gulf of Rosas to Cadaques, a round trip of around thirty miles. It was a pleasant town and we had plenty of time to explore and shop. As we gathered for the journey home, I recall seeing things that our lads had bought to take home as presents: perfume for Mum, cigars for Dad and wine for other relatives. Next morning at inspection there were some very sickly looking boys. 'Something we ate, Skip,' they groaned. I knew differently. Some of the presents would never make it home!

On the way home we camped one night at the tiny principality of Andorra, wedged high in the snow-swept Pyrenees between Spain and France. With a population of only 25,000, it seems incomprehensible that, as I write, this small country finds itself playing England at soccer. As we drove through Andorra la Villa, the capital, looking for a campsite, we were puzzled by pedestrians who kept waving. Some time later we would discover that their public service vehicles looked very much like our motor home and that they had been hailing us to stop.

Philip and Margaret Hutchings with their children seeing off their uninvited overnight guests heading home from Spain.

After the long drive through France, we arrived tired and in need of a good wash at the home of Philip in Hertford (see p.23). This would be my last camp on the continent with Senior Scouts. Of all the camps I've been on, the two in Spain were more like holidays, because the boys were young adults, really, and there was no pressure to do test work.

Chapter Fifteen

Two years under Canvas

It sounds quite unbelievable, but when you add up all the summer camps, Jamborees, Easter, Whit and weekend camps I have been to in my life, it does add up to almost two full years! For many years I would not just take my own Scouts or Senior Scouts camping, but also help David and Terry with their camps, thus leaving no time for personal holidays. I have chosen to describe two camps in some detail, partly because they were special, but to no small degree because I have an excellent aide-de-memoire in Syd Turney's interesting and detailed log books. I will finish the chapter with the earliest of these two and also the most local, because, looking back, I now realise that it is not always the duration of the camp or indeed the distance from home that determines its success.

The first of the two came about through a connection made at the Welsh Jamboree in 1961, when I befriended two Irish Scouters who suggested that we bring 1st Kendal Scouts to Ireland for their summer camp. The possibility of this happening required serious thought. The logistics involved in taking the whole Troop abroad were complicated, but above all we would need a strong team of Leaders. At one of our monthly Leaders' meetings six Leaders promised support and I was left to make preliminary enquiries. I was due a holiday and I decided that I would go to Ireland to explore the possibilities. I contacted the two Irish Leaders and a few weeks later we met at Enniskerry close to Powerscourt, where the Irish Scouts had a large campsite within the grounds. The 100 room house was owned and occupied by the Slazenger family, best known for tennis racquets. I was impressed with the campsite, but still a little worried about it all. However, at the home of one of my newfound friends, and after a few glasses of Guinness, things began to look more plausible. When they offered help with our camp programme and told me about some of the activities they would be able to arrange for us, I became quite enthusiastic and went as far as to visiting the food suppliers in the area of Powerscourt. Actually, I only had to visit one shop: M. Tallon and Sons, Grocers, Provision and Hardware Merchants, Flour Meal, Bran and Corn Stores. They advertised daily deliveries and assured me that they would be glad to help and were looking forward to receiving our orders. When the proprietor said that he could also supply sunshine for the week, I was completely sold on the idea of an Irish camp.

After months of planning and preparation we assembled at Kendal Railway Station late in the afternoon on Thursday 2nd August to catch the 6.05 train

David Parker, Bob Meakin, Barry Link and Barry Levens cooking on an open fire.

Tim Molloy and Roy Clement cooking twists.

for Liverpool Docks. Our party comprised twenty-one Scouts, twelve Senior Scouts and seven Leaders. British Railway excelled themselves. Trains were on time, reserved coaches were at our disposal and to complete an excellent journey, all our equipment, which had travelled as advance luggage, awaited us at Princes' Dock. Travelling overnight on the M.V. Munster was far from ideal. Inside, the boat was packed and every seat was taken. The best option seemed to be the hard planks of the upper deck, where at least the air was fresh. We had nine hours ahead of us, and to keep warm we huddled together like sheep in a storm. Syd writes, 'How long can nine hours be? Almost an eternity without the saving humour of our race! Imagine a frozen, snoring Scoutmaster being roused from his slumber by a small Scout requesting that his false teeth be taken care of, lest they get broken in the throng!' Were we happy when the boat slipped into the Dublin docks the next morning!

The transition of boys and equipment went smoothly, and before long we were all seated in the Powerscourt Arms Hotel, enjoying a hearty breakfast of bacon, egg and sausage, bread and butter with marmalade, and tea (5 shillings a head – or 25p in new money). Incidentally, the hotel proprietor was a Kathleen Tallon – perhaps that explains why the aforementioned Mr. Tallon had recommended breakfast at this establishment. He did not, however, immediately deliver on the weather! The boys just managed to get their tents up, before the heavens opened! The Leaders had only got one tent pitched, so all seven of us squashed together and sat there for three hours, wondering if the rain would ever stop.

The next day we did see the sun, in amongst the showers, and we managed to set up a camp that found favour with the Camp Warden, who lived with his family in a cottage at Powerscourt, but was actually a solicitor in Dublin. The Seniors walked the $4\frac{1}{2}$ miles to see and photograph Powerscourt Waterfall, at 398 ft. (120 metres) the highest waterfall on the British Isles. After the Scouts had enjoyed spending some of their pocket money in the shops of Enniskerry, they prepared their tea, while some of us Leaders went off to enjoy the hospitality of my Irish Scouter friends. Terry, who had misunderstood the invitation and thought we were invited to a meal at a local hostelry, was more than a little disappointed to find himself having a drink in a Scout Hut. The activities they had arranged for the Scouts, though, were first class.

As part of their Queen's Scout training the Seniors had to go on a Venture Adventure Journey, dealing with a variety of incidents on the way. Our Irish friends had devised a course more challenging than any I could have come up with. First the lads treated injuries in a car accident, simulated of course.

Setting off on twenty-five mile adventure hike in Ireland; Eldred Himsworth, Ian Shepherd, Ian Harris and Alan Barker.

Arriving back, tired and wet.

They then had to follow a tracking course, reading signs along the way before, finally, tackling a commando course. They crossed the river by rope-bridge (blind-folded), negotiated an electric fence, crawled through a long culvert into a river, waded along the river and climbed a rope to a bridge 15 ft. (4.5 metres) above.

One day we all enjoyed a coach visit to Dublin, complete with a City Guide who pointed out every building of note from museums to churches to government buildings. After a hot lunch, the boys had another opportunity to hit the gift shops. One boy in particular impressed Syd with his thoughtful gift buying. He writes, 'Andrew Yare has been working over the past year to save up enough money to pay for this camp and also to purchase gifts for his family. He is indeed a remarkable lad and a very useful Scout in the camp kitchen. If all the boys did more at home, camp cooking and washing up would be much easier.'

The highlight of the Dublin visit was undoubtedly the afternoon visit to St. Michan's Church and Vaults (A.D. 1096). For one shilling you were able to go into the vaults to see bodies in a wonderful state of preservation, even though they had not been embalmed. For an additional sixpence you could shake the leathery hand of one of the bodies, and most of our lads were happy to shell out the extra!

The day was rounded off with a swim in the sea at Bray before returning to camp, tired and happy. The Leaders were no less satisfied as they had managed an excellent meal in the Wicklow Hills Hotel while the boys swam.

During the camp eight Seniors completed their 25 mile Venture hikes and three members of the Scout Troop their First Class 14 mile hike. Having so many Leaders in the camp (and especially my former Seniors John Barber, Mike Allen and Mike Sagar, who had become Leaders) enabled the Scouts to make excellent progress. Many badges were earned and tests passed. It also allowed us 'older' Leaders (I was 33) to take time out for a little exploring on our own. We managed a trip out where we caught glimpses of the old Ireland – for example the pub without electricity where we had our lunch.

Before leaving we presented Mr. Scott, the Camp Warden, with a thank-you gift of a two ounce tin of Kendal tobacco ('Bob's'). He gave us a glowing report and told us that he hoped we would return in the not too distant future. The camp ended as it had begun at the Powerscourt Arms Hotel, this time for tea. The two Dublin Scouters, who had come to see us off, were duly thanked for all their help in making the camp a success, and then

Morning inspection. Skip Head springs a surprise.

Tired chefs after cooking a meal for Scout Dignitaries on the Isle of Man at 1994 camp. The menu was Melon with prawns and Marie Rose sauce, Coq au vin, and fried bananas with a Mars bar sauce. Chefs Huan Quayle, Howard Pimblett, Ben Allen and Mark Holden are pictured with assistant cooks Grant Walling and Kirsten Cannon.

it was time to leave the Emerald Isle! The ferry ride back was, if anything, more uncomfortable than the trip out as the ferry was much more crowded. The rain kept pelting down and the tarpaulin covering the aft deck, which we had been so happy to see, turned out to be a mixed blessing. It would occasionally shed its load, depositing vast amounts of water onto the deck, so that we got soaked from beneath instead of from above! The duration of the trip was also longer as the ferry called at Birkenhead to unload cattle!

It was a sorry looking lot that disembarked the train at Kendal Station some hours later, but when we had all recovered, we agreed that 'the Irish Camp' would be remembered fondly!

I am not sure how it happened, but as the years went on we ceased to make as much use of the local area for camping as we had done in the earlier years. After trying camps in various locations, we settled into a pattern of alternating between three sites: Marlow on the Thames, Aldwark near York and Walesby near Nottingham. The three sites offered quite different opportunities, so in his time in the Scouts a boy would have had a variety of camping experiences. Walesby is a huge site belonging to the Scout Association. It has a rifle range, an archery range, a climbing wall and a swimming pool – all very popular with the boys, but, of course, the use of these is limited as many groups share the facilities in any given week. In comparison, Aldwark is a very plain site with few facilities other than a toilet block with hot showers, but its situation on the river Ouse gives the opportunity for messing about on the water! We would build rafts, have canoe tug-of-wars etc. Because there were fewer organised activities, it was a more relaxed camp. The campsite we used at Marlow was in a beautiful situation, right on a curve in the river, so naturally canoeing was one of the main activities here.

At least one day of each summer camp was always spent away from the site. All Scouts and Leaders would get dressed in their uniforms, which since the arrival at camp had been hanging neatly on a rail in the supply tent, and head for civilization. As mentioned earlier, the outings from the Marlow camp would go to London where we would visit either Wembley Stadium or the R.A.F. Museum in the morning and the Science Museum in the afternoon. After tea at B.-P. House, we would walk to Earl's Court to see the impressive Royal Tournament. It would be a very tired bunch of boys – and Leaders – who returned to camp late at night. Another day we might go to Windsor to look around the town and visit the castle.

From Aldwark we would have an outing to the nearby R.A.F. Station at Linton-on-Ouse. On another day we would all head into York where tickets

Pioneering project at Walesby camp, 1991.

Fun on the rope bridge

would have been booked for the Yorvik Viking Museum and – in the early days - also for the Castle Museum. This visit became an option when we realised that most of the boys hardly looked at any of the exhibits, but seemed to have a race to see who could get through the building and out the other end the fastest. There would always be some free time and the option of visiting the Railway Museum.

The Walesby camp offered the opportunity to go horse riding, although nothing as exciting as our earlier Appleby experience! There might also be a visit to a big mining museum near Nottingham, the highlight being a guided tour of the mine.

Certain elements, of course, were common to all the camps: early morning inspection, competition between Patrols and, not least, 'Mum's cake'. Some boys gained great popularity because their mothers were fantastic cake makers – Stephen Horn's mum, Marjorie, from Natland stands out in my memory. (She, incidentally, had been one of Barbara Hughes' many helpers in the Cub Pack). One job which, even in the latter years, was my speciality was helping the boys construct quite elaborate pioneering projects with ropes and spars, block and tackle. It might be a pyramid signalling tower, a ducking stool or a lookout lift around a tree. The biggest project I ever undertook was at Walesby in 1991. It was an elaborate structure, with a ladder to a lookout post, a swing at one end and a gigantic rope scrambling net which, hammock-like, could support up to a dozen boys!

Over the years, the Leaders of 1st Kendal have got camping down to a fine art. Our equipment is excellent and bears little resemblance to that of the early years. The Patrol tents are Nijers and the Leaders sleep in frame tents. The equipment and food store is a 12 ft. square marquee. When Skip Bainbridge is along, there are even electric lights. The kitchen equipment is adequate and both cooking and washing up is made easier by having a big boiler so hot water is always 'on tap'. Camp routines are well established: Skip Keegan's creative camp letter to the parents, where the boys just have to tick choices, is a must as is the tuck shop run by Chris Head who is also quartermaster and camp banker. Planning and running the activities is shared between all the Leaders, but the over all responsibility rests with Scout Leader Stuart Laurie who takes care of morning inspection, giving out trophies at the end of camp and much more!

I must just mention the sad demise of the old-fashioned campfire. Many sites do not allow open fires, but even where there is a fire pit, it goes largely unused. It seems that neither Scouts nor Leaders nowadays are keen to sing campfire songs or stand up in front of their peers to perform a sketch! As long as I was involved, we did try, but when you are the only Leader willing to lead a song, it is hard going. Having said that, there was one young camp assistant who was very good at getting the boys to sing, a former 1st Kendal Scout, who continued to attend the summer camps after having left for university. He was Grant Walling, grandson of Stan Walling, the man who could get 110 boys and their Leaders to sing out on a stage in front of an audience of nearly four hundred.

Forgive me if I again give in to nostalgia about my childhood in Natland, but it seems a fitting way to end the book. When I was a boy there was so much to do, and the area between Hawes Bridge and Robin Hood Island was pure magic. (Every time I drive down Hawes Lane and see the signs 'No Trespassing' and 'Keep Out' by the entrance to Hawes Wood, I pity the children of Natland today, who are deprived of this magical land)! I was in awe of the River Kent at Hawes Bridge as it passed silently over huge limestone slabs. These could be very slippery and my mother had warned me never to go near them. I never did! Hawes Wood was nothing less than a dense jungle, impenetrable in places by swamps. There were no crocodiles, but on a number of occasions I saw otters and I once saw a snake(!!) - I was sure it was a rattler! Here we found the very best wood for making bows and arrows. I recall replacing the leather band on my wide-brimmed Scout hat with a strip of birch bark from a tree in the 'forest'. We would emerge from the wood, blinking in the sunshine, to find ourselves in rich, green pastures. The river at this point became wide and lent itself to swimming. Beyond the swimming area, well trodden animal tracks led to the wonderfully named Robin Hood Island. Standing between high banks, its shape resembled a ship and it was well covered with an assortment of trees. Gaining access during periods of high water was impossible, but when the river was low we could wade across. For a boy with just a smidgeon of imagination it could become almost anything! As the waters united beyond the island, the river gathered speed before crashing down between steep rocks to enter another wooded area. It was here in the 19th century that a weir diverted water away to a mill-race to power machinery in the gunpowder works. Through the kindness of farmer Mr. J. Howson, this was the location for our Whitsuntide camp in 1963.

One of the obvious advantages to choosing a site close to home is that you can do a lot of the preparation of the site ahead of time. On this occasion, the weekly Troop meeting on the Monday before the camp was spent at the site with the boys digging their rubbish and grease pits, making their fire places and marking out their tent and kitchen positions. On the Thursday the Seniors visited the site and put in some excellent work erecting palatial toilets in the woods (with a stile to get over a barbed wire fence) and constructed a coracle ferry to the water supply on the other side of the river. The final touch was a flag pole!

The following letter had been sent to the parents ahead of time:

Whitsuntide Camp, Friday evening 31st May to Tuesday midday 4th June.

Dear Parents,

We are holding a camp for the Boy Scout Troop at Whitsuntide and would like every one of our boys to be there. Our campsite on the banks of the River Kent between Hawes Bridge and Robin Hood Island affords wonderful opportunities for real Scout adventure, and those attending can be sure of a grand time. Our programme includes swimming, bridge building, rafting, aerial runways and general pioneering.

On Whit Monday at 7 p.m. we shall be holding a barbecue and campfire to which you are warmly invited (Coffee and hot-dogs 2/s; bring your own mug). We would like parents to visit us on this day, not Saturday or Sunday. Otherwise we should spend the weekend brewing tea.

The boys will be working in patrols (i.e. doing their own cooking, making their own rafts etc.) and it would be appreciated if each Scout could bring a cake with him to camp to be shared among his patrol. Please do not give the lads piles of sweets or chocolates. They can have fruit.

Please send the camp fee of £2.5.0d (£2.25).

As part of the preparation, the Westmorland Gazette van had been pressed into service to carry all our camping gear, and on the Friday night the boys just managed to beat it to the site. Setting up camp was soon done, leaving only a few gadgets to finish the next morning. When the gadgets were finally passed, the Seniors, Ian Harris, Eldred Himsworth, Ian Shepherd, Deryk Tebay, Brian Elshaw and David Atkinson, who were staying in the camp, took over. They gave an excellent display of camouflage and stalking. The highlight was provided by Eldred who swam down the river, keeping pace with the walking Scouts, his head hidden behind a floating branch. He remained undiscovered until he swam into the brilliant sunlight where his arms and legs, moving under the water, gave him away. Deryk Tebay demonstrated the use of clothing camouflage when he lay amongst the rocks in full view, without being spotted. A half mile tracking trail was laid in the woods for a number of Second Class aspirants, but this did not prove very successful as all got lost! The afternoon's instruction was rounded off

Syd Turney in coracle on the River Kent near Sedgwick.

Crossing the weir below Robin Hood Island.

by the Seniors giving a demonstration of crawls and methods of observation used in stalking.

During the following swimming session, much enjoyed because of the intense heat, a number of boys passed their 50 yard swim towards their First Class – surely a much more memorable way of passing the test than doing $2\frac{1}{2}$ lengths of the old Kendal Swimming Pool.

After tea the Seniors organised a number of games and it was here that Kevin Turney's nose got in the way of a flying rounders bat, resulting in a couple of days in hospital.

Drinking water had to be collected by coracle from a spring on the opposite bank. Never have I seen boys so keen to volunteer to fetch water!

On day two the Seniors again took over the programme. They had laid a Patrol observation trail through interesting country, finishing with a walk across the top of the weir by the old millrace. From there the boys had to cross a monkey bridge, across a deep gorge to Robin Hood Island. From the high point of the island, an aerial runway stretched across to the mainland. Only two boys failed to make the trip, but fortunately only their pride was hurt. Two of the very young Scouts, J. Duckett and R. Clement, tackled the crossing like old hands, while Terry Swainbank narrowly missed a bath when he lost his footing at the high end of the runway. At the conclusion of the trail, the Seniors gave an exciting display of shooting the rapids in coracles. Deryk Tebay and Mike Murphy proved to be the experts; the rest had a refreshing dip!

The day ended with games and prayers, except for the Patrol Leaders who set off on a night hike through Levens Park, along the canal and back to camp. Unfortunately all did not go according to plan. After getting lost in the park, they finally arrived back at 2 a.m. – to the relief of Terry and me who had been out looking for them.

The last afternoon was spent on a new monkey bridge over a deep pool and on an aerial runway which dumped its victims in the middle of the river. It was great fun! The evening barbecue for the parents was a resounding success, except for the boys who had to go without their hotdogs as so many guests showed up!

Thinking back now, I sincerely hope I thanked those Senior Scouts enough. They truly did a magnificent job and showed what the Scout Movement is all about – older boy teaching younger! I am pleased to see in the 1963-

1964 Year Book of the Westmorland Boy Scout Association, that their exceptional qualities and accomplishments were recognised by the editor of the national magazine, 'The Scouter', a man by the name of Rex Hazlewood. He writes:

'*Have been reading with much delight the log books, illustrated with drawings and photographs, of the 1st Kendal's Mitchell and Scott Patrols' Pathfinder Expedition in the Ardnamurchan Peninsula last Easter. 'The district of the expedition', as one log began, 'is wild, desolate and rugged countryside. It has a tremendous potential for Scout Training as when a Patrol is taken and left there by itself, it has to operate as a complete and independent unit. Each member realises that he is an essential part of the small community. The Scout senses a deep responsibility on himself for the well-being of the Patrol, which forms a good, reliable character and a tolerant disposition.'*

The logs included reports on agriculture and industry, wildlife and the weather and were at times brutally frank:

'*The innocently named Claish Moss was, in fact, a treacherous bog that psychologically tortured the mind and magnified the inevitable aches and pains to an alarming extent. The morale was quite low, and we mistook crows for vultures waiting for us to collapse and die. We stumbled over clumps of grass, which often moved, for about two miles...*'

Throughout, the logs shone with humour: '*I let Alan and Elsh divide the cheese, but nobody knows why Elsh and Alan were still eating their 'fifths' of the cheese long after the rest of us had finished ours*'; *or:* '*We ate a kind of tea consisting of one can of stewing steak, one bar of chocolate, one Swiss roll and one orange each.*'

Rex Hazlewood's final paragraph reads - and I must confess to a sense of pride as I read it again after so many years:

'*There is plenty of wonderful Scouting happening today – enlightened, enterprising, adventurous. These are the days we shall dream about!*'

Chapter Sixteen

Into the Second Century we go

As 2007 approaches, and with it the Centenary of the Scout Movement, it is good to know that the 1st Kendal is still thriving. It consists of a Beaver Colony, a Cub Pack and a Scout Troop, which alone has about forty members.

When I turned seventy, I stopped going to the weekly Scout meetings, but I still keep in touch and know most of the people involved as Leaders. The only one I don't know personally is Brian Harper, who runs the Beaver Colony with the help of parents. (I realise that I have not mentioned Beavers at all in the book, as they are a much later addition to the Movement. They are six and seven years of age).

Soon after his eighth birthday a boy joins the Cubs, where he remains till he is ten and a half. Ashley Henderson is in his twenty-third year of leading the Cub Scout Pack, the same one he attended as a young boy. The fact that he has managed to keep the same assistants for many years is a testament to his approach and ability as a Leader. It is an impressive record that, since Barbara Hughes came on board in 1959, there have been only the two Akelas! Barbara's granddaughter, Karen Tansley, nee Hughes, has been Assistant Cub Leader since her school days, carrying on the family tradition. Alan Muil has been with the Pack for fifteen years and Phil Bonney since his boys, who are now both adults, were Cubs.

Stuart Laurie was an assistant with the Cubs before joining the Scouts about fifteen years ago. He took over running the Scout Troop from Roger Downing in 2002. (Roger is now Group Treasurer). Stuart is assisted by Chris Head, who has been with the Group since he joined the Cubs in 1974, and by Peter Allen and Don Quigley who both became involved as parents and later became warranted Leaders. At the top of the tree as Group Scout Leader is Tim Keegan, a post he has held for thirty-seven years!

The senior section of the Movement is now called Explorer Scouts and boys join at the age of fourteen and a half. Kendal has a joint Explorer Scout Unit which meets at the headquarters of 4th Kendal.

It is wonderful to see that so many dedicated people are still involved with 1st Kendal, but the Group will need new, younger Leaders if it is to carry on well into the second century of Scouting. Nothing would give me more pleasure than to see some of our former Scouts come back as Leaders. I can highly recommend it as a hobby and - after all - IT IS ONLY FOR A COUPLE OF HOURS A WEEK!

1st Kendal Scouts - Aldwark 1990

Back Row: David Rider, Geoff Bainbridge, Jim Cannon, Chris Head, Trevor Hughes, Tim Keegan, Alistair Burgess, Nicholas Allen, Scott Pearson.
Fourth Row: Jonathan Keegan, Grant Holden, Andy Banks, Adam Burgess, Paul Thompson, David Rae, Roy Blaydon, John Egerton, Paul Stelfox, David Jackson, Wayne Oldham. Third Row: Ken Banks, Ian Greenhalgh, James Longden, Matthew Wood, Nicholas Perry, Chris Cunliffe, Chris Lowe, Jeremy Fielden, Charles Longden, Chris Bland, Philip Herd, Richard Daws, Iain Worsley, Jamie Lawson, James Andrews. Second Row: Grant Walling, Jacqui Holt, Daniel Egerton, Thomas Waters, Paul Durrant, Simon Bayliss, Amy Thomson, Rachel Woolley, Kate Brambles, Simon Whittaker. Front Row: Michael Thorp, Ben Allen, Gareth Denny, Edward Nash, Anthony Sunter, Adam Sedgwick, Peter Andrews, Howard Pimblett, Andrew Clarkson, Lawrence Bates, Neil Lancaster, Matthew Sewell, Tim Nelson, Nicholas Rigg, Michael Firth, Mark Holden.